'From the editor of *thewalk* comes [...] message that is real, gritty, relevan[...] book has been needed for a long ti[...] lads everywhere.' Tim Jones, youth leader

'Has this book been written just for me? Many of these chapters applied to my life, the things that I am getting wrong and the areas that I struggle in. My passion is to be more like Jesus and this book has helped me to understand how God wants me to do that. I would encourage any lad to get *Rad Lad Livin'*.' Chris Harvey, student

'Mark's vulnerability spoke to me and deeply impacted my life. It is so refreshing to see a "named" Christian speaker write with honesty about their life and what they get wrong. Jesus' vulnerability and honesty changed a generation; this book could do the same.' Sam Peterson, aged 17

'As a church leader, the big bruva accountability set up in this book seems spot on to me. Real application will only take place if followed up. I would encourage any church leader to order copies for "big bruvas" and the lads in their youth group alike.' Paul Holmes, church leader

'Let's be honest – some people will not like this book! Why? Because it is honest and takes a straight down the line approach to the fact that we desperately need to change areas of our lad lifestyles. It is for this same reason that this book will be a best seller. It will change the life of every lad that reads and applies its message.' Andy Richards, student

'So a lad picks this book up and what does he do? He jumps straight to the chapters that contain the words "porn", "wankin'" and "lust" – we all struggle. These chapters really helped me to deal with this issue in my life and now my big bruva is keeping me on track too! Lads, let this book challenge you!' Simon Johnstone, aged 14

'Jesus was gritty. *Rad Lad Livin'* is gritty. Jesus challenged lives. *Rad Lad Livin'* challenges lives. Jesus impacted a generation. *Rad Lad Livin'* could possibly do the same.' Isaac Roberts, youth leader

'I was asked to comment on this book in order to recommend it to others. I didn't expect it to challenge the very core of my lifestyle. Is this a good book? Ask my girlfriend what she thinks about the changes it has made in my life!' Oli Grey, aged 20

'This book is biblically accurate, honest, vulnerable and gritty. If after reading this book lads aren't filled with a passion to change their lives and be uncompromising and radical in the way that they live for Jesus, not much else will change them.' Andy McPherson, youth leader

rad lad livin'

MARK BOWNESS

survivor

Survivor is an imprint of
KINGSWAY COMMUNICATIONS LTD
Lottbridge Drove, Eastbourne BN23 6NT, England.
Email: books@kingsway.co.uk

Book design and production for the publishers by
Bookprint Creative Services, P.O. Box 827, BN21 3YJ, England.
Printed in Great Britain.

This book is dedicated
to Auntie Meryl, whose godly lifestyle truly taught
me the meaning of the word 'radical'.
You are missed.

contents

thanks

Vikki, 'You mean everything to me.' Thank you for supporting me throughout the writing of this book, with editing, wisdom and love – we got there. You are the strength behind this wannabe 'rad lad'.

My family: Mum, Dad, Chris, Caroline, Molly, Jon, Sara, Steve, Emily. I love you. You never give up on me but keep pushing me on. Thank you for your support, encouragement and love in all that I do even when it gets tough.

Tom Blundell, my best mate. You know what you mean to me. I love you. Ben Taylor, you challenge me from a distance. I miss you.

Papa C., Jase B., T.J. AKA Soulcry, you guys inspire me.

The Wyatts: Baz, Mephib, Steph, Geoff and Joe. I love you guys being in my life. Your support amazes me. Thank you.

Mark and Annie Porthouse, for reading, commenting and challenging. You are great friends.

Angie Brett, your addition to the walk has made it what it is. I can't thank you enough.

John Pac, Dave Roberts and Richard Herkes. Thank you for releasing a vision. You have enabled me to capture my 'one shot'. I respect you.

Dave and Pam Bishop, you know I respect you and love you. To all at YCC: we have a church to call 'home'; you guys rock!

There are heaps of lads across the world who challenge me, inspire me and who I can call friends: Will Thompson, Steve Hart, Joe Attard, Dave Bentley, Dunc and Ky Usher, Andy Rowlandson, Andy Frost, Gerald Coates, Larry Norman, Neil Godding, Adam Dyer, Bob Chew, Josh Gibbons, Rob McAvoy. And the rest – you know who you are.

Jesus, the ultimate rad lad. Only you know what you have done in my life. I remain humbled and in awe. I love you.

safe!

So why is Mark's best mate writing the foreword for his book? You may think that this is a ploy to tell you how great *Rad Lad Livin'* is, and Mark has bribed me with a few beers to do so. That isn't true. The deal is that I know Mark very well, I am the closest lad to him who can tell you whether he really seeks to live out the message in this book, and to be honest – he does!

So, let's talk about Mark. Well, he isn't perfect, and he will be the first to admit it. I could tell you about the countless times Mark has come to me apologising for not living out some of the stuff he encourages lads to live out in this book. That is the point: Mark is real, honest and vulnerable and that's why *Rad Lad Livin'* will impact your life.

Rad Lad Livin' is the perfect manual to help any lad move forward in God and deal with serious lad issues that, let's face it, need challenging and changing in all of us. This book has been needed for a long time – real lads looking at real lad issues. God is raising up a generation of lads who are passionate for him, who are willing and ready to sacrifice their lives to get it right for him, bringing him glory. *Rad*

Lad Livin' inspires you and motivates you to be part of that generation.

Rad Lad Livin' has come out of Mark spending time with lads across the UK dealing with issues in their lives, from lust to identity, from brotherhood to homosexuality – making this book practical in its nature and real in its content.

Rad Lad Livin' is written with honesty. Mark lets you into his life and recounts stories that are painful to tell yet crucial to hear. Mark has grappled with some biblical issues in order to present them in a real and relevant way, then sprinkled it with stories of past and present, making this a challenging, interesting and significant book for any lad to read.

Rad Lad Livin' has challenged me and I am certain that it will challenge every lad who reads it and will affect a whole generation of lads who choose to apply its message to their lives. Imagine a generation of rad lads changing lives and communities for Jesus. So that's Mark and me down for rad lad livin' . . . anyone else?

T.J.

keepin' it real

Lad culture is hitting an all-time moral low. Images of football hooliganism are rampant across our television screens and in our newspapers, with blokes beating up other blokes for a 'laugh' or more importantly to act as a self-protective mechanism to mask their own fears and insecurities. Lads parade an 'I'm a man!' badge on their t-shirts, coupled with the strangest of male-animal-like grunting noises and beating of chests, as a mere attempt at running from the real issues they need to deal with, which have remained for so long hidden beneath the surface. We hear countless stories of lads who 'have fun' and sleep around. The result? Teenage pregnancy and sexually transmitted diseases are on a dramatic increase. We enjoy the bloke banter: the heroisms, the footy, flirting and the first alcoholic binge as we struggle to prove that we really are a 'man'. However, at some point our eyes are opened, we start to talk to lads in the youth group and we slowly discover that they feel the same way – they are trying to prove themselves too! This 'masculine image' is forced upon us by the media and we buy into the propaganda in a futile attempt to chase what can never be caught, an image that doesn't exist. The further you enter this spiral, the more you are left feeling hurt, confused and broken. Something has to change.

I have spent time having a 'one to one' with many lads who have had to deal with their addictions to porn, lust and masturbation. I have been in a room talking to a teenage lad who was in tears because there wasn't a part of him that he liked. I have talked to lads who have battled with being a man of God in today's lad culture. As I talk to these lads, I do one thing; I point them to the character and person of Jesus Christ, a man who lived out true radical lad culture. Dude, I am not trying to make a heap of lads into a bunch of sissies, but Jesus embraced a godly lad character along with care and compassion. Jesus violently turned the tables in the synagogue as he protected his Father's house, and he was also full of love and kindness as he lived out his life as a servant King. I am convinced that if we start to live out a rad lad lifestyle, then as lads we can usher the presence of God into our communities, our schools, our relationships, our places of work and our homes. Rad lad livin' could change the course of history and result in a reverse of this moral trend!

Before I started this book I thought that radical meant 'extreme' – to be out evangelising, to see people healed and miracles take place, to see the masses become saved through our words and actions. Dude, that isn't what radical means. As I have prayed, researched and written, it is clear to me that to be a rad lad means to surrender your whole life to the will of God, to allow him to be in control, despite your own emotions, what your mates are doing and the way it has always been done. Rad lad livin' means listening to God and obeying his voice alone – that's radical!

The word 'radical' means from the root upwards. My

desire is for this book to change you from the root upwards, to deal with every bloke issue that lurks inside you, to get right to the root and tackle the most sensitive, the most challenging and the scariest issues that you will ever have to face as a lad in the twenty-first century. It is a challenge to be honest and open with ourselves, to get real about the way our lifestyle has become, but as we are honest and as we check out what God's word says about lad culture and apply this to our own lives, we will be transformed by the renewing of our minds. There are no quick answers. Philippians 2:12 says that we should work out our own salvation with fear and trembling. This book isn't about answers; it's about ideas and themes that will push you into God to figure out what he has for your life. Bro, get into God and you will develop further into the journey of being a rad lad!

This book details an honest personal journey – the way I have messed up, the things I have got wrong and the struggles I have faced. It is as we are real with each other as lads that we will see a freedom in our struggles and situations. At the end of each chapter a 'Sort it out' section will offer hard-hitting suggestions on making practical changes in your own life.

You will also find a 'Big bruva' section at the end of each chapter. I would like to encourage you to find an older bloke who you respect as a rad lad and go through the 'Big bruva' section with him, meeting up regularly. Your 'big bruva' will help you to keep on track with your rad lad livin' lifestyle.

Finally, this book is full of respect to rad lads. We have chatted to rad lads who have made some changes in the areas of lad culture that we are tackling – use their stories to inspire you, to motivate you and challenge you to be all out for God in your own life.

A health warning must be applied. This may be the scariest journey that you will have faced to date, but as you apply what God says to you through this book, your life will be changed for ever. The decision is yours.

Mark Bowness

1
not guilty!

Heart pounding. Parents gone. Glance around – no one looking. The sweet shop is full of sweets and those foolish Christians have left an 'honesty box' for me to put my money in as payment for any sweets I take. Yeah, right! Born yesterday? My entrepreneurial mind is racing. This is a chance not only to gain free sweets, but also to increase my holiday spending money by taking dosh from the box. Wicked! Opportunity seized. I walk off with one pocketful of money and another pocketful of sweets, plus a big grin for thinking I'm so clever. No one saw!

Driving back, I had more money than I had gone with and it was only a matter of time before my parents found out. I tried to blag an answer, but deep down they knew that I had stolen a heap of money from a Christian hotel whose owners had offered more trust than I had honesty. I only remembered this sinful occasion as I started writing this book and I must stress that, much to my embarrassment, I have since confessed to my parents and have also sent a letter of apology to the hotel along with a cheque to cover what I stole. A serious rad lad lesson. Once you have recognised that you have done something wrong, sort it out, confess your sin and go and apologise to those you have offended or sinned against. Try to make things right.

> Therefore, if you are offering your gift at the altar and there remember that your brother has something against you, leave your gift there in front of the altar. First go and be reconciled to your brother; then come and offer your gift. (Matthew 5:23–24)

Challenging stuff. It isn't easy, but it is the rad lad biblical thing to do. My holiday money-making idea is just one example of the heaps of stuff that I have got wrong as a Christian lad. As I share my stories with you, I am not trying to brag in an attempt to gain respect but am simply being honest in the hope that they will challenge you to seek to be more like Jesus. We are going to deal with sins in our lives; we are going to face them head on in order to see change and become a blatant, all-out 'rad lad' in the kingdom of God.

Mission Impossible, starring Tom Cruise, was a wicked film. You remember the line, 'Your mission, should you choose to accept it . . .' In the film, Cruise's character, Ethan Hunt, tackles his missions head on with one aim – to overcome and win. I offer you a mission, should you choose to accept it! Your mission is to tackle the sin in your life – to tackle it head on, to get right with yourself, with others and with God. Deal with the stuff that really affects you – the swearing; too much drinking; the way you treat women; the areas in your life that you have so desperately tried to get right but have failed; all the stuff that God has been trying to discipline you over but you have simply ignored him. God is disciplining you; he is making you aware of the stuff that he doesn't like and this is churning you up inside, but keep it real, bro – this is what the Bible says:

> My son, do not make light of the Lord's discipline, and do not lose heart when he rebukes you, because the Lord disciplines those he loves, and he punishes everyone he accepts as a son. (Hebrews 12:5–6)

God loves you. You are his son, he is moulding your character to be more like his, and he is getting rid of the rubbish in your life that repeatedly tears you up inside. When Ethan received his mission, he was told that the tape would self-destruct in ten seconds. Maybe you have come to the point where it is now or never. You've got to accept the mission head on and tackle this stuff, or you will self-destruct. Let's accept the mission together. Looking at the sin in our lives is positive stuff because it encourages us to correct ourselves and change. Anything that helps us to live a rad lad lifestyle is good, despite painful disciplining by the hand of God.

The importance of obedience

There is a calling over my life. I am a husband, a son, a brother, an uncle, the editor of *thewalk* magazine, and I run a national ministry. I am also now an author! I am not telling you all this to score points or to gain respect. These roles and responsibilities equal my calling; the very 'stuff' that God designed me, Mark Bowness, for. God has things for us all to do; he wants to take our lives on one exciting roller-coaster ride of a journey. The ride may get bumpy, it may turn you upside down, it may even make you feel sick, but at the end you will be well pleased that you jumped on the journey with God. There is a calling on each of our lives, despite our abilities or inabilities, no matter what we think of ourselves, no matter what other people think of us or have said to us. You sitting here, reading this book . . . you have a calling, a God-appointed mission for your life. How do I know this? The Bible tells me:

> I knew you before you were formed within your mother's womb; before you were born I sanctified you and appointed you as my spokesman to the world. (Jeremiah 1:5, TLB)

God doesn't simply have stuff for Jeremiah to do; he has a purpose for each one of his children. We live in this crazy world that 'judges books by their covers'. If you are larger than the average dude, you are rated as ugly. If you can't play sport, you are not respected as much as those who can. The same zany attitude exists in the Christian world too. Some have this understanding that if you preach, if you lead a church or run a ministry, then you are more important than people with other callings. Rubbish! Being obedient to God is important; the content of the calling is irrelevant! What counts is that you are doing the job that God has called you to do.

The responsibility that is placed upon my calling is the same responsibility that is placed upon yours – whether you are at school or university, whether you work in the pet shop down the road or are training to be on your local footy team, whether you are a youth leader or a cell leader, whether you are a boyfriend or you are single, at this moment in time these are your callings and you have a responsibility to work hard and to live out a Christ-like lifestyle in all that you do. It's your obedience to your call-ing that counts!

A time for change

Before I started to write this book I had many sleepless nights. Why? Because I realised the great importance and the magnitude of the responsibility of writing a book that would teach and encourage lads to live a better lifestyle. Condemnation raced through my mind. Who am I to teach lads how to live a better lifestyle? What about all the stuff that I have done wrong? The apostle Paul tells us that he is the sinner of all sinners:

> Here is a trustworthy saying that deserves full acceptance: Christ Jesus came into the world to save sinners – of whom I am the worst. (1 Timothy 1:15)

One day I will chat to Paul – I think I win the award for 'worst sinner'! I struggled while preparing to write this book. Surely the sin I've amassed in my life doesn't qualify me to teach others. The knowledge of my sin was being used as a barrier to stop me walking into my future. Our past can rob us of the plans that God has for us because when we feel guilty we can't function. We can feel so bad, so hung up about the aspects of our lives that don't please God, that we don't continue in our calling, we give up on God and ourselves. Has your knowledge of your past sins held you down like an anchor, keeping you from moving on with God? It's time to change.

Two types of sin plague my head – past sin and current cycles of sin. Past sin, not the little stuff, but the big stuff looming in my mind that Satan chucks up every now and then when things in my life seem to be going good – stuff like stealing money, lying big time, doing things with girls that I shouldn't have done. I am sure you can come up with your own list! The second lot, current cycles of sin, is the stuff that you ask God to help you to stop: you think it's gone but no, here we go again . . . that stuff! Many blokes now will be thinking of the same cycle of sin. Can't guess? Wankin'! We will be dealing with this in a later chapter, but for lads tackling this area in their lives it can be tough. The sins that we have committed, both past and present, can chew us up and leave us feeling low and distant from God. Sometimes I get before Jesus in an attempt to say sorry and move on, but I can't let go of the fact that I have let him down, so I run away and do something else to keep my mind occupied. The longer I take to sort out the stuff that I have done wrong, the more guilty and condemned I feel, and I end up missing out on my relationship with God.

Tackling the guilt and condemnation

Over the years I have learnt to tackle properly the guilt and condemnation that comes from messing up as a Christian. First, as far as God is concerned, all sins are the same, they are wrong. Therefore, whether we have slept with a girl or sworn at our parents, beaten someone up or stolen some money from a Christian hotel, sin is sin. This is important to understand because we only feel guilty about the wrong that we consider to be big in our lives, not the little stuff that we do each day – we disrespect our parents, we tell 'white lies', we don't honour God in our school work, college work or careers. If these sins are just as bad as each other, then in our guilty and condemned state, strictly speaking we should feel guilty about the whole lot – and man, that is a lot of guilt and condemnation! So, either we hold on to all this guilt or we let it all go. It is easier to let go of the stuff that we don't view as being 'as sinful', but God wants us to let go of it all. We sometimes get so caught up in Christianity that we have a dumb blonde-type moment and forget what the whole deal is really all about. Let's read what the writer of the Psalms has to say:

As far as the east is from the west, so far has he removed our transgressions from us. (Psalm 103:12)

Jesus died on a cross in order to take away the sin of the world, to remove it as far as the distance from one end of the horizon to the other. That's the whole deal! When we come to Jesus in repentance, in that split second he has forgotten our sins. Jesus does not continue to hold that sin against us, and therefore there is no reason for us to hold our sin against ourselves. On the cross Jesus cried out, 'It is finished!' Our guilt, our shame and our condemnation have finished because Jesus knows all our sin and has forgiven it all.

Jesus explains a top scenario in Luke 17:11–19. Ten lepers saw Jesus from a distance and called out to him to have pity on them. Jesus had compassion for these lads and told them to go and see the priest, and as they did this they were healed. One of them got excited about the fact that he was clean and came back and threw himself in thanks at Jesus. (Well, wouldn't you?) Jesus asked this man where the rest of his mates were, the ones he had also healed. They hadn't returned, but Jesus told this rad lad to go on his way, explaining that his faith had made him well.

I used to be like one of those lads, unclean in sin. I used to call out to Jesus, who would always forgive me and make me clean, but I let my sin entangle me and keep me away from God, leaving me feeling guilty and condemned. Dude, I am learning to be like the leper who, having been made clean, did not stay away but came running back to Jesus in thanks and praise. Jesus died for you on the cross once and for all; for all sin, past, present and future – the big sin and the sin that we see to be little. Jesus died for it all and as we call out to God for forgiveness for the wrong stuff that we have done, we need to have the faith that he has made us well – and then what? Simply return to him and fall at his feet in praise and worship.

Let go of your past sins and your cycle of sins. God has forgotten them and you need to forget them too. I want us to continue and explore together what it is to be a 'rad lad' for Jesus Christ, moving on in our callings and in obedience. However, we can only do this knowing that 'it is finished' and that the guilt and shame have gone. Remember, the apostle Paul, Mr so-called chief-of-all-sinners, says:

Therefore, since we are surrounded by such a great cloud of witnesses, let us throw off everything that hinders and the sin that so easily entangles, and let us run with perseverance the race marked out for us. Let us fix our eyes on Jesus, the author and perfecter of our faith, who for the joy set before him endured the cross, scorning its shame, and sat down at the right hand of the throne of God. (Hebrews 12:1–2)

Sort it out

- Spend time before God and ask him to bring to memory the sin in your life that you need to deal with.
- Grab a concordance and look up some specific sins that you struggle with, then check out the Bible references to see what God has to say about them.
- Spend time in prayer and ask for God's forgiveness. Remember, once he has forgiven you, 'It is finished!'
- Praise God for his work on the cross and the fullness of life that this has enabled you to enter into.

Big bruva

In this chapter I mentioned the cycles of sin that we get entangled in, be that smoking, drinking too much alcohol, sleeping around, or many others. Once you have repented of these sins in your life, find the courage to chat to your big bruva about them. Talk them through with him, ask him to pray with you and make sure that he keeps checking up on you in these areas. Some of these sins are harder to combat than others, but with God and a big bruva on your side you will kick these cycles.

Guilt can hit us in two forms.

First, there is false guilt or condemnation. This is when we experience guilt because maybe we feel we are not praying or reading the Bible enough. Or we conclude that we don't love enough. It is linked to feelings of inferiority and ineffectiveness in our Christian lives.

Second, there is real guilt. In other words, we *feel* guilty because we *are* guilty! This occurs when we really do tell lies, sexually lust after others, drive a car irresponsibly, get drunk or gossip.

False guilt has to do with unfulfilled expectations based upon unreality. For example, not praying enough – how much is enough? We may feel ineffective in evangelism when we are not evangelists, but simply witnesses.

Real guilt comes from real sin. In the West sin is linked to immorality, so sleeping around is immoral behaviour. In the Eastern Church sin is seen as damage we do to ourselves and others.

Confession (1 John 1:5–10) and repentance (Acts 3:19) are the way through. Confession simply brings things out into the light. It enables us to see a thing for what it is. Repentance is turning away and choosing another way to live. The Spirit of God will always help us do that.

Ultimately sin is against God. He cannot be indifferent about it. But amazingly, he gave us his Son to make a sacrifice for our sin, enabling us to confess, repent, believe and be saved, both now and in the age to come.

Gerald Coates,
Team Leader, Pioneer

2
Jesus – a rad lad role model

The latest *Matrix* film hits the cinema and you are there! What a film! As the credits roll, you are left gob-smacked, still in your seat wondering what it would be like to be in Neo's shoes. Who wouldn't want to be Neo, even if just for a day? Neo, of course, flies. He sees speeding bullets in slow motion. He walks on air, flips, twirls and punches his rivals with deadly force, even though Agent Smith just laughs in the face of death! Your mates have already headed for the exit, spilling the remains of the popcorn over the chairs on their way. The lads shout for you to hurry up, but you are left with a dream, a dream that your lifestyle could be like Neo's too. Now wouldn't that be cool?

We don't need another hero!

Our society is full of heroes. We have present heroes like David Beckham, Robbie Williams, Richard Branson or Tiger Woods. We look up to heroes of the past, like Kurt Cobain and John Lennon, or we respect fictional heroes like Neo, Terminator or Batman. We don't need any more heroes.

Bro, having heroes like these is nothing more than fictional fantasy. How can Neo help you with peer pressure? How can Beckham improve your quality of life? How can Terminator help you deal with your daily struggles? The answer? They can't!

We often fall into the trap of seeing Jesus as a fictional character, but he wasn't. Jesus actually lived, died on a cross, rose again and paid the price for our sins. Jesus was the Son of God who came to this earth in human form, performing miracles, chatting to sinners and loving the lost. He was tempted in every way and yet was without sin, fully qualified to understand what you are going through every minute of your day. Jesus is a rad lad role model I would like to point you to continually! The Bible doesn't say that you should have Terminator, Beckham or even Bart Simpson as your role model. Unsurprisingly, it points you to Jesus:

> Love the Lord your God with all your heart and with all your soul and with all your mind. (Matthew 22:37)

Or roughly translated, 'Make Jesus your role model.' I want to encourage you, as a rad lad, to strive to be like him alone.

Jesus – irrelevant?

Something has gone drastically wrong. It's serious. We have made Jesus irrelevant to the rest of the world. Jesus was the most radical man ever to have lived on this planet, living an up-for-it lifestyle that was centred on making God known through completely loving and serving people and bringing the power and presence of God into every situation that he faced. What a rad lad! We have got it wrong and this desperately needs to change, as the image of Jesus we portray is putting the world off the very thing that they are desperately seeking. Bro, let's do it; let's check out the true image of Jesus and present that truthful image to the world around us, radically impacting everyone we meet. It's certainly time for a change, and this is my call for us rad lads to get on with it! Are you with me?

Hell-condemner, happy-clappy, wimpy or cool?

OK, so let's deal with the image of Jesus. It is something that us lads need to get our heads around. The truth is that the image we have of Jesus is created by the way those around us represent him. There are two stereotypes of Jesus that we have presented to the world. First, there is the guy who preaches on the street corner shouting that 'the wages of sin is death', condemning everyone to hell, which is exactly where his tweed jacket and 'Jesus sandals' should be! Passers-by moan, shout and swear, as you walk past with your face hidden, praying that your mates won't mention the fact that you are 'one of them'. Second, there are the guys at church. You know, the happy-clappy husband who has a happy-clappy family, who always smile in that annoy-ing 'I'm a Christian' sort of way, and yet church rumour tells you that they have a 'desperate' new problem every week, and actually aren't all that happy!

Jesus has been presented to the world as a 'wuss' – as some nice, smiley, happy hippy dude, a Mr Bean sort of character who is well wimpy and goes about telling everyone that he loves them. Trust me, this is not the Jesus I know. However, there is another twenty-first century image of Jesus that has started to surface; a myth that I want to blow apart. This is the 'cool' Jesus. We meet these cool Christians at the summer festivals, after they have saved up all year to buy the latest gear, camping in their newest, brightest trainers, clean new footy tops, and newly launched hairstyles that all the girls love. This 'cool' and 'trendy' Jesus is not the real Jesus I know either. We all as Christians reflect Jesus Christ, but our view of Jesus, and therefore our reflection of him, is clouded by the sin that is in our lives.

> Now we see but a poor reflection as in a mirror; then we shall see face to face. Now I know in part; then I shall know fully, even as I am fully known. (1 Corinthians 13:12)

God's people can only reflect him in part. As I encourage you to make Jesus your number one role model, you need to seek to have revealed to you who Jesus actually is. If you have a role model, then you will check out as much information on them as possible. Girls are more blatant than us lads, buying the girly mags for the posters of Justin Timberlake that fill every inch of their bedroom walls; checking out all J.T.'s interviews to ensure that they are up to date on his latest likes, dislikes and tour dates. Bro, we are just the same in our own little way! I love Beckham, I think he is a footballing genius, I have read his books, I follow his games and when he comes on TV I subtly have one ear focused on whatever he is saying so that no one around me can quite tell that I am absorbed. But I am!

If we have a role model in any aspect of our lives, we want to know all about them and we get absorbed in them. We need to get absorbed with Jesus. I don't mean that we should find horrific posters of him in outdated Christian bookshops and pin them up on our walls. I mean we should become serious about getting to know him. We need to spend time in prayer, reading the Bible and worshipping him. As we do this, we will get to know him and we will be able to become more like our role model, changing our lives and radically impacting the lives of those around us.

Compassion, servanthood and force

OK, so you are asked to describe a 'typical lad'; what comes into your head? My top five list of words would probably be sport, girls, beer, sex and a macho image. I certainly would not think of compassion and servanthood, although using the word 'force' would certainly save my credibility! The words that we use to define a 'lad' are based on the images around us, what we see on TV, the way our mates are, and the way we believe we should act as lads. Bro, this is completely wrong. As Christians we need to see a complete change; our definition of a lad should be characterised by the nature of Jesus, the ultimate rad lad. So, I think of words to define Jesus: compassion, servanthood and force. You may not think of these three words being put together in the same sentence, but as we take a look at the rad lad role model of Jesus, we will see how he lived out these three characteristics perfectly. It is these character traits of Jesus that we need to understand and see become reality in our own lives.

Compassion for smelly people

I remember when I used to go with a team of students to spend time with the homeless people in our city. The first thing I remember was the smell of unwashed bodies and stale alcohol. It was disgusting, and on many occasions made me seriously want to puke. Nevertheless, we wanted to go and show the love of God to these people. On one particular occasion I was with an older homeless guy who really did smell and was looking old and frail. My instant reaction was to walk away – anything to get away from the smell. However, as I watched him I saw tears in his eyes and sadness in his face. I sat down next to him as he began to explain to me the story of his troubled life, of how his wife had died, of how his children did not want to know him and of how he struggled daily to find the will to even exist. On top of all this he had not eaten for a week and understandably was very hungry! While I chatted to this guy I was moved with compassion. I wanted to help him in any way that I could because I saw him as Jesus did – as a beautiful man of God whom he loved dearly and for whom Jesus had died. My compassion drove me to action and I became a servant to him, befriending him, collecting food to feed him and blankets to keep him warm.

Some people smell. It is true! This could be the literal smell of unwashed homeless people who beg for spare change on the streets. It could be the 'smell' of something not being quite right with a person's character, or it could be the stench of sin on lads around us that makes us turn our noses up and walk on. But Jesus didn't do that and neither should we. He didn't turn his nose up at them or walk away, and he didn't gossip to his mates about the state that person was in. Jesus went to them, had compassion on them and sought to do something about their need. Jesus was filled with compassion for people.

When he saw the crowds, he had compassion on them, because
they were harassed and helpless, like sheep without a shepherd.
(Matthew 9:36)

Compassion is understanding the suffering of others and
doing something about it, in the same way that Jesus did.
Stop. There you have it! As you start gaining the heart of
God and having compassion for people, that's when you
choose to do something about it, and become a servant. As
you gain compassion for God's people you naturally take on
the role of a servant, and on occasions these acts of servanthood involve using force!

Let's go back to the homeless guy. As I sat listening to
this guy with tears in his eyes, there were also tears in mine.
He had lived a sad life and his current situation was a result
of circumstances beyond his control. As I was filled with
compassion, I wondered what Jesus would do. He would at
least have provided food and warmth, so that's what I did!
However, as I took on the role of a servant I had to use
force: I had to track down food and blankets, I had to seek
help from my church, and I had to use force in order to
carry on serving this guy, even though my mates questioned
my actions and wondered why I wanted to spend time with
an old, smelly, homeless alcoholic.

Jesus had compassion for people because he understood
the heart of God. It was this compassion that led him to
serve the people around him. From turning bread and fish
into a banquet or befriending and spending time with a tax
collector, to challenging the sin in the life of the woman
caught in adultery, he served! Bro, when did you last show
the compassion of God to people? When did you last serve
someone or use godly force to change a person's life? What

did you do when the kid at school was being bullied or the homeless guy on the street asked you for change? What actions did you take when even the Christians around you were not being compassionate towards the lost and the unsaved? I bet it is probably time for change in your own life. It certainly is in mine!

Miracle maker

What a film! Have you seen it? *Miracle Maker* is set in Israel and follows a sick girl named Tamar. She is drawn to a carpenter who performs miracles, turning water into wine, seeing sick people healed and miraculously enabling people to walk away from the sin in their lives and believe in themselves once again. That radical bloke is our man, Jesus! He really did all that stuff! Vicky Beeching has written a great song with lyrics that pick up on a verse in the Bible (Hebrews 13:8) and exclaim, 'Yesterday, today and for ever, you are the same, you never change.' You can't talk about the character of Jesus without talking about the miracles that he performed, and as Vicky reminds us, God never changes and therefore he still performs miracles today. If, as rad lads, we are seeking to have Jesus as our role model, then we need to seek to bring the miraculous power of God into everyday situations.

A boy with crutches

God had been challenging me on the subject of healing, so I spoke about it to around 200 young people at a youth event. In my humble opinion, the talk went well, the crowd were amazed and God's presence was there as I closed with a prayer that God would encourage us to pray for healing in the lives of the people around us. As soon as the meeting ended, the group parted just like the Red Sea, and through the middle of the room a boy with crutches walked up to me. The room fell silent and I started to pray that God would open a hole in the ground to swallow me up. As I looked at the desperation in this boy's face, I knew what was coming and I knew God was challenging me on the subject of my own talk. The boy shouted out for all to hear, 'If your God is a healing God, then let's see him heal me!' It would be wrong for me to share with you the swear words that raced through my head as I realised that this lad of 17 was not even a Christian. OK, I thought. Compose yourself. God can handle a broken leg. We will pray for him and tell him that sometimes the healing of God takes a while to actually occur!

'What's the matter?' I asked.

The boy replied, 'I have cancer. The doctors have given me a few months at the most to live.'

Cancer! I thought he had a broken leg! The crowd was gazing on and the room was silent. There was nothing I could do but trust God. He got me into this situation and, as far as I was concerned, he had to get me out – after all, it was his reputation at stake! I turned to the group and asked them to come around this person, to pray for his healing together, and that is what we did. I am blown away to tell you that this lad was completely healed of cancer and is now a Christian. Nice one, God! However, not all stories end in this way. I have prayed for people who have not been healed. God does not heal everyone, but I have learnt one important rule. The deal is that in the Bible we are told to lay hands on the sick. *The Message* puts it this way:

These are some of the signs that will accompany believers . . .
they will lay hands on the sick and make them well. (Mark
16:17–18)

I have begun to realise that it is a biblical command to pray
for the sick, and therefore that is all we can do; the rest is up
to God! Bro, let's be like Jesus. The next time your mate
tells you that he is not feeling well or you overhear a stranger
explain that he's not feeling too good, why don't you pray
for that person's healing? This stuff isn't easy, but if we want
to be more like Jesus and live a rad lad lifestyle it is what
both you and I should be striving for.

Average, ordinary, everyday miracles

The very lifestyle that Jesus lived was miraculous in its
nature. Jesus touched and changed every life he encountered. We have Christ in us and therefore we should be
doing the same. Whose life have you changed recently? We
can change people's lives by asking them how they are feeling when they look down. When they have no friends, we
can ask them whether they want to hang out with us. Every
day we can be a miracle in a person's life; it takes a rad lad
to do that.

It was our first Christmas together and finances were very
tough. Vikki was upstairs sitting on our bed crying before
God, gutted that we could not have some decent food at
Christmas time. God looked on Vikki's tears as prayers. The
next day she was at the local supermarket buying basic
foods. As she got to the check-out, a lady from our church
appeared and explained that she had been meaning to
contact us as God had told her to buy some food for us, and

she encouraged Vikki to go back through the shop and fill up her trolley. We were amazed! A few days later a couple in our church, who we didn't really know, turned up on our doorstep with two Christmas hampers of special food. We ate and ate that Christmas and had plenty left over. These people had performed modern-day miracles in our lives, all because they were willing to listen to God, obey and act. There are many unanswered prayers lost in tears in your community. I want to encourage you to take a look at how you can be a modern-day miracle in the lives of the people around you.

You can't manufacture the character of Jesus

Unfortunately, you can't just force out these character traits in the same way that some actors can turn on the water-works from deep within. Jesus spoke out against the Pharisees who tried to manufacture a godly lifestyle:

> I've had it with you! You're hopeless, you religion scholars, you Pharisees! Frauds! Your lives are roadblocks to God's kingdom. You refuse to enter, and won't let anyone else in either. (Matthew 23:13, *The Message*)

Jesus rebuked these men and told them that they were frauds. The Pharisees tried to reproduce the lifestyle they knew they should live, rather than having the character of Jesus flow out of their lives because of their passion for God. We all have times when we fall into this trap. It is particularly easy if you have been brought up in a Christian family to try to manufacture how you should act, as opposed to following the rad lad lifestyle of Jesus because you have a

deep and intimate relationship with God. Out of his relationship with God, Jesus was obedient and submitted to all
that his Father asked him to do. The result? Crowds daily
drew near to Jesus and their lives were changed.

If we are seriously going to be a bunch of rad lads who
have Jesus as our role model and turn lives upside down, we
have to get intimate with our Creator to ensure that our
lifestyle is for real. I would like to encourage you to make
time for God each day. Spend time getting into his presence,
by praying, reading the Bible and singing away to a worship
CD. A favourite worship leader of mine sings, 'Lost in
wonder, lost in love, I'm lost in praise forevermore.'

Bro, both you and I need to get lost in the presence of
God. Matthew 12:34 tells us that out of the overflow of the
heart the mouth speaks, and I am sure that it is the same
with the character of Jesus. Out of a deep relationship with
Jesus, his character, the fruit of the Spirit, will flow through
our lives: love, joy, peace, patience, kindness, goodness,
faithfulness, gentleness and self-control. It won't be a stress,
strain or struggle, and it certainly won't be manufactured.
The character of Jesus will come so naturally to you that it
will surprise you. Your life will be changed, as will the lives
of those around you. I want to encourage you to seek to live
out the rad lad character of Jesus in your own life, based on
the intimate relationship with God that we are working
towards. Go for it!

Sort it out

- Make space in your life daily to spend some time with
  God. Ask him to give you his heart of compassion for
  those around you.

- Seek daily opportunities to serve people, performing acts of compassion and modern-day miracles.
- Ask God to reveal to you those around you who need prayer for healing, and commit time to praying for their healing. Go and ask them if you can pray for them.
- Make a list of all the modern-day miracles that have happened to you and take time out to pray and thank God for each of these.

Big bruva

We have looked at Jesus' character, compassion, servanthood and force. It is not always easy to put these into practice in your own life. Spend time with your big bruva who knows your character, and ask him to show you how you can take steps in your own life to be more compassionate, be more of a servant and use godly force. It will be easier to implement some character traits than others, so ask your big bruva to encourage you in these areas.

If you're going to be a Christian you have to dedicate your life to Christ. You have to make choices that you believe Christ would want you to make. Should I steal or not? This would be an easy choice for most of you to make. Should I go out with this girl or not? Well, that might be more difficult to determine. But God will help you make each decision if you pray and ask him to. Taking the wrong path even in small matters will take you miles away from the place where God was leading you. Is your life in God's hands – or yours? Are you going to sit on the throne, or are you going to get off and let Jesus occupy the throne of your heart?

The Christian life is not a simple matter of obedience to rules. It's not merely a matter of choosing light over darkness or siding with good over evil. You still have a much more important challenge in your life. Avoiding wrong is not the hallmark of a godly life. You must also do what is right.

You wanna be a rad lad, eh? Try obeying Jesus. That's pretty revolutionary in this world you live in. Try affecting the community around you by showing love, kindness and generosity to people. Tell them about Jesus so they'll know that your feelings come from somewhere special and resolute.

They'll definitely not think you're smarmy and wet if you live your Christian life with power and resolve. Some may think you're idealistic or outdated, but give them time and they may come to understand that you're centred and strong.

Do not merely listen to the word, and so deceive yourselves. Do what it says. Anyone who listens to the word but does not do what it says is like a man who looks at his face in a mirror and, after looking at himself, goes away and immediately forgets what he looks like. (James 1:22–24)

Larry Norman, singer/songwriter
www.larrynorman.com

3

it's not about me – or is it?

In bed again. Should be at school. Haven't been now for about four weeks. I spend my days in bed watching daytime TV and trying to figure out what is going on in my life. Life isn't going anywhere. Have you ever been bullied – physically, mentally and verbally bullied to the extent that you have secret desires to end your own life but you wouldn't, you couldn't, so you find a different form of escape? Blokes don't have anorexia, do they? I do. I don't eat food, surviving mostly on hot chocolate with cream, trapped in insecurities, fear and an inability to love myself. I hate looking in the mirror because I see something ugly, something spotty, something unattractive inside and out. I see me. I see a wimp and a weakling who allows lads to torment him and hurt him, who lives in fear of those he used to call his friends. I don't love myself.

That was my life. I am from a family of six kids with loving parents, all of whom I love hugely. But as a teenager I went through a dark, depressing time that shaped and formed my life. I was never very good at sport and I tried to get out of these lessons in any way I could: accidentally forgetting my kit, suddenly developing a fake asthmatic attack . . . anything! Nevertheless, there were times when I had to take part in a sports lesson and changing into my PE kit filled me with dread, especially if it was football we were playing. We would walk onto the pitch and two team captains would be chosen to pick their teams. The best football players and the most popular lads would be picked first and the whole embarrassing process began. The players who were not so bad would be picked next. As my face started turning bright red and the numbers of people left dwindled, it was guaranteed that I would be last, left standing there like a lemon and met with a heap of booing from the team unfortunate enough to get me. No one wanted me on their team. Why? Because if a football ever came towards me I would run in the opposite direction! I hadn't got a clue what to do with it! I wasn't good at football and I wasn't the most popular lad in my year. This inability to play sport became the basis for widespread bullying and tormenting that lasted a number of years and resulted in me becoming seriously depressed.

Reflection in the mirror

My complete dislike of myself was also fuelled by the reflection I saw in the mirror, encouraging me to stay away from mirrors altogether. I hated my spotty face. I had tried every available medicine to get rid of those spots, but nothing worked. Things got worse and I became more and more insecure. I eventually developed an eating disorder, seeking attention. I was driven by a need to feel loved. For many months I stayed off school, ill in bed, my body wasting away because I wouldn't eat. I look back now and think of the few occasions when I wanted to commit suicide and get it all over with. At that time my eyes were set upon myself; I didn't have the heavenly perspective of the beauty and purpose that God has created and designed in my life. This combination of external bullying and abuse and the internal agony of my view of myself became very painful, keeping my focus on me rather than God. I was certainly unable to keep a focus on those around me whom I, as a Christian, was supposed to love. Bro, if we can't love ourselves, we become self-absorbed and unequipped to love those around us. My diary entry from one of those days states:

> I hate me. I look in the mirror and see this thing that I hate. As someone who loves God I am supposed to love people around me, but how can I show love when I am unable to love the thing that is supposed to show it? God, please teach me how to love me.

The bullying, the acne, the anorexia and the unhappiness became focal points for care and concern from those around me who did love me. I craved the attention, but inside I was slipping away. Things had to change, otherwise my life would have been pretty much over before it had even begun.

We bottle it up

Over to another fave film of mine, *Good Will Hunting*. Will Hunting (Matt Damon) is a genius, but he has chosen a job as a cleaner at a top American university. Will's incredible photographic memory means that he is more intelligent than many of the rich, well-educated students at the uni, but he does not have any great ambitions because he fails to see the potential and worth that is deep within. At 20 years old, the effects of Will's past are pretty similar to mine, ruled by the way he was treated and bullied by others when he was younger. In Will's case his view of himself is dominated by the way his father would beat him, scarring him both physically and mentally, reducing him to a belief that he has no place of worth within society. Will reaches a critical point when his therapist, played by Robin Williams, challenges and confronts him with his past. In another session, his therapist repeatedly tells Will, 'It's not your fault,' and Will is reduced to tears. This is crunch time for Will as he breaks free of his past and is able to start accepting himself, and so move on into his future.

Just like Will Hunting, we have a perception of ourselves based on our own experiences, insecurities and fears. Many of us hide this view, good or bad. Bottling things up is the blokey way to deal with things, right? We tell no one, we hurt inside, get angry, and beat ourselves up. We lack any confidence to love ourselves, let alone love the lost. Some of us bottle this stuff up until we self-destruct and find a negative and harmful way to deal with the anger or hurt, whether it be sleeping around, drinking, smoking, taking drugs, being violent or harming ourselves, just like I did. Are you at this place? On the verge of self-destruction? Already crossed the line? How do we sort ourselves out?

Commanded to love

Back to my story. You may be wondering how I got out of my bedridden, depressed, near suicidal state. After months in my bed, eating little food with a body wasting away, God began to speak to me. I'd had one day too many in bed, one day too many feeling sorry for myself and getting angry, one day too many of not eating and of watching my body go to waste, and I'd had enough. Once I reached this place, I called on God to help me out, to intervene in my life, and he did. I started to read the Bible and God spoke to me through some incredible Bible verses. In this particular verse, Jesus was questioned by one of the Pharisees who tried to trip him up. This Pharisee pointed to all the laws, rules and regulations in the Old Testament and he asked Jesus which of these was the most important. Jesus replied:

'Love the Lord your God with all your passion and prayer and intelligence.' This is the most important, the first on any list. But there is a second to set alongside it: 'Love others as well as you love yourself.' (Matthew 22:37–39, *The Message*)

In my dark and desperate place, God spoke. First command: love God, love him with everything that you have and are. Second command: love others as well as you love yourself. I was always taught, as a kid, that this verse meant we should treat others the way we would like to be treated. That's cool, but it is not the message that is hidden in the heart of this verse. Jesus says that the first important command is to love God; the second command is to love ourselves and then to love others in the same way that we have love and respect for ourselves. God spoke to me very clearly. Jesus commands us to love ourselves – deeply! Images may now be jumping in your head of endless *Pop Idol* wannabes who tell the judges they are going to be the next best thing – despite their inability to sing, their tragic dance moves and Simon Cowell's desperate pleas for them to leave the stage! Many of these wannabes are learning to deal with pride and arrogance, which is actually based upon their own insecurities. There is a difference between loving yourself, having self-respect, self-worth and loving what God has created, and pride and arrogance which does not come out of a love for God.

Blokes loving themselves? Strange! Bro, we don't talk about this sort of stuff. Each of us deep down has a desire to be confident with the bodies that we have, to be pleased with our character and to be aware of those bits about us that we don't like, in a way that we can handle rather than in a way that causes harm and frustration. Being a rad lad is to acknowledge that we need to deal with stuff we don't often talk about, so let's start to deal with it here and now!

The lad for the job

Why should we love ourselves? Dude, let's check out Moses, a biblical *Good Will Hunting* equivalent. God sees the potential in Moses as a rad lad, so he meets with him at the burning bush to share the plans he has for his life, to lead the children of Israel into the Promised Land.

It's fantastic, never-seen-before, explosive, Hollywood-style, history-making stuff! God has not met with a human being in this 'we are in the same space together', loud audible voice sort of way since Adam and Eve in the Garden of Eden hundreds of years previously. However, there's a problem. Moses can't see the rad lad potential that God can see:

> But Moses said to God, 'Who am I, that I should go to Pharaoh and bring the Israelites out of Egypt?' (Exodus 3:11)

Moses heard his call from God, but the things he did not like about himself stopped him believing he could be the lad for the job. Moses knew himself, his failings, and the bits about himself he didn't like: just like Will Hunting, just like me, just like you! As he stood before the burning bush with God mapping out the plan he had for his life, there was one specific concern flying around Moses' mind:

> Moses said to the LORD, 'O Lord, I have never been eloquent, neither in the past nor since you have spoken to your servant. I am slow of speech and tongue.' (Exodus 4:10)

Moses was aware that he wasn't 'eloquent' in his speech and questions raced through his mind, like 'How am I going to lead a nation who can't understand me?' Moses was focused on his natural inabilities; the things that hindered him from achievements and accomplishments. He was focusing on the things that had probably been the butt of other people's jokes. Many had probably laughed at Moses' slow speech, whether this was to be cruel and spiteful or simply to get a laugh. To Moses it didn't matter; the fact was, he had convinced himself that the way he spoke would never allow him to achieve anything in life. As God asked Moses to lead the Hebrew nation into a new future, Moses' view of himself and the task was moulded by negative words said over him in his past. Surely God must have got it wrong, Moses thought. Surely this was a recipe for great disaster rather than great success.

Bro, we need to learn to love ourselves, first because God commands us to, and second because God wants to use us, like Moses, so we can walk into the future that he has for us. The way that we view ourselves has stopped many of us from reaching our full potential in Christ. If we are to live a rad lad lifestyle and have our relationship with Christ as a strong foundation to help us truly impact this world, our view of ourselves needs to change.

We too are called sons

I truly began to love myself again once I realised that God loved me enough to send his Son to die on a cross for me. It is crucial that we begin to understand this. 'For God so loved the world that he gave his one and only Son . . .' (John 3:16). God loves us enough to send his Son to die for us. Once we begin to see ourselves from this viewpoint our perception is changed. If God says that we are worth it, then we are. Full stop.

As I was in my bed one night, unable to like myself, God encouraged me to check out Matthew 3:17 and hear the words that he had spoken over Jesus: 'This is my Son, whom I love.' We too are called sons of God (1 John 3:1) and I figure that God would treat all his sons the same, making the same proclamation over your life and mine: 'This is my son, whom I love.' As I started to think about these verses, to take them on board and believe them to be true, I started to fulfil the first command that we talked about earlier, to love God with everything that I am and have. This provided a basis for me to start to love myself.

Next I had to deal with me. It took time. I had to be honest about what I didn't like about myself; some of these things I had to change, and others I had to accept. But again, God provided me with a verse from the Bible, from Genesis 1:27, which explains how God has made man in his image. You and I are made in the image of God, and in this way we are special, unique, and we have an image to be proud about. As I started to understand these verses, I started to love myself and to move forward in loving the lost and getting excited about the plans God had for my life.

A time for change

Nevertheless, there was one big hurdle that I needed to jump. In *Good Will Hunting* we see that Will's therapist knew there was a time when Will had to stop thinking the way he did about himself. In my own life, sitting in my bed, anorexic and depressed, a point came when something had to change. As we get back to the story of Moses, we will see a common theme occur. Remember that Moses was standing before the burning bush unable to receive the plan that God had for his life. Moses was concerned about his natural inabilities, worried that he wasn't eloquent in speech. Let's see how God responded:

> The LORD said to him, 'Who gave man his mouth? Who makes him deaf or mute? Who gives him sight or makes him blind? Is it not I, the LORD? Now go; I will help you speak and will teach you what to say.' (Exodus 4:11–12)

Moses' inability to accept himself meant that he could not move forward in the vision that God had given him. Instead he moaned and complained and tried to convince God to choose someone else. However, God was on Moses' case, as he knew that he was the rad lad for the job. Moses complained further:

> Then Moses said to God, 'Suppose I go to the People of Israel and I tell them, "The God of your fathers sent me to you"; and they ask me, "What is his name?" What do I tell them?' God said to Moses, 'I-AM-WHO-I-AM.' (Exodus 3:14, *The Message*)

God was telling Moses, 'Enough! Get on with the job.' Will Hunting was told, 'Enough! Get over your past,' and a time had also come for me when things had to stop. My problem was that I liked the attention which came from people knowing that I was ill and bullied. The way that I did not love myself enabled me to be the centre of the very thing that I craved for – love.

We have two options. We can remain in a place where we don't deal with our insecurities; an easy choice as it means that we don't have to face the real us, the things that we don't like and even hate about ourselves. If we don't face up to these things, we are also left chasing the things that will make us feel loved – the sleeping around, the alcohol, drugs and all the other stuff – and we continue running from God. Or there is the second option, the better option. We can work towards loving God, finding our foundations in him, and as an overflow we can begin to love who we are.

Dude, this is a challenging choice, as you will have to change some things in your life and stand up to your mates who will encourage you into heaps of temptations. However, the result of making this choice will enable you to grow as a rad lad, to love God, to love others and to be released into the amazing plans that God has for your life. Despite the pain, I chose the second option and I thank God every day. My life could have been over before it had begun.

I challenge you to take the second option, to get over it and face up to yourself, the things that you do and don't like, and to discover who you are in God's eyes. I can guarantee that this is a choice you will never regret. Go for it!

Sort it out

- Take some time out and write down the top five things you like about yourself and then take the courage to write down the top five things you don't like about yourself. Praise God for the things you like and ask him to help you with those you don't.
- Take a look at the Bible and see what God says about the areas you don't like about yourself. Ask your big bruva to help you.
- Think about the things that enable you to feel loved. Ask for forgiveness for the things that you do in this way that are wrong, and ask God to help you to change.
- Take some time out to ask God to reveal to you his love, and delight in the fact that he does!

Big bruva

When you have made a list of the things you don't like about yourself, be brave enough to share it with your big bruva and ask him to pray for you. There will be a change in the way you see yourself. As you think about the things you do to make yourself feel loved, be brave enough to share these things with your big bruva too. Ask him to help you stop and to challenge you to change in these areas, helping you to become a rad lad.

OK, it's confession time! I was a sulky teenager! Nothing unusual there, eh? Except I was a world-class sulker engaged in marathon sulkathons! I was angry, but instead of exploding in rage, I would quietly seethe and make those around me suffer. If people said the wrong thing I'd be gone – huge door slam, out the house and down the street in a strop!

My insecurities began in my family situation, where I struggled to live up to the successes of my two older brothers and felt constantly compared, never favourably. It was only when I became a Christian at the age of 17 that I began to deal with this. When I was stomping down the street, I always hoped someone would run after me and persuade me to come back. Man, I must have been hard work. To be honest I just felt worthless. I believed that I could never please God and that I was always a disappointment to him. I felt that nobody loved me and if, horror of horrors, they ever discovered what I was really like, then I would just die.

How did it change? A guy called Terry Virgo preached on 1 Corinthians 1:25–31 at a big Bible meeting when I was a student. Terry showed me that if I felt weak, useless, unloved and thick, then the Bible says I am top of the list to qualify to be used and loved by God. I made choices and changed my thinking, beginning with how I felt about others. Instead of worrying whether others loved me or not, I created a new mantra. 'It doesn't matter what you think of me, God loves me.' Slowly, as these truths sank in, God made me secure.

Mike Rimmer, radio broadcaster and journalist
www.crossrhythms.co.uk

4
lad culture

It is Bournemouth Uni, 1999: nightclub, banging tunes, dance floor and bright lights. At least I think this is where I am. The tunes, the lights and the people are all blurring into one as the effect of my fifth vodka starts to kick in. I suppose the three (or was it four?) pints of beer may also have had something to do with it! It has been a good night, I think. I kissed one or two girls – don't remember much, though! I say goodbye to the lads with a blokey grunt or two – some of them are still on their feet, well just about. I make my way out of the nightclub on my own; if I stay any longer my mates will realise that I can't take my drink and I will never hear the end of it. Don't want that. I walk on, stumble, fall over, pick myself up again, and on we go. I manage to get into my room after fumbling for the key, dropping it, picking it up again and dropping it once more. I am in. I lay my head on my pillow, jump up, am sick in the toilet, well half in the toilet, at least. I put my head down again and fall asleep to a spinning room and fear of being sick once again.

You think that story is cool? It isn't. Why? Because I spent stupid amounts of money on alcohol just to try and fit in with a crowd and to impress some lads I didn't really like anyway! Not to mention how ungodly it is to snog two or three girls in one evening. Foolishness! But we're all guilty. Whether it is the alcohol, the clothes or the particular subculture that we are in, we are too busy trying to impress those around us to find out who we really are. Every lad in your subculture is like this, all trying to impress each other, all trying to fit in. That is what lad culture is really about.

Adidas, Sambas, 'blades or Dr Martens?

What do skaters, 'bladers, townies, moshers, goths and sporty guys all have in common? No, this isn't a joke! They all want to belong. You attach yourself to a particular subculture that enables you to feel part of a community; you exist within a particular group of people that helps you feel that you belong. Bro, we all want to belong, and that is OK! You will see sporty lads at the gym together or on the footy pitch. You will see goths around town in black clothes, black hair and possibly some eye shadow. You will see townies with their latest gear on, looking trendy, and skaters probably skating in the local supermarket car park from dusk until dawn, getting the latest trick completely spot on. We all want to be around mates we get on with, who are into the same sport, fashion and music and who see the world from the same perspective as we do. Great stuff. No problem. But there *is* a problem with lads getting involved with subcultures, with mates and doing stuff that means they gain approval in men's eyes but not in God's. Dude, you do this. We all do, we are human. We just need to tackle the areas we find difficult and make sure they are pleasing to God. OK, now that we have brought him onto the scene, what does the big guy say about this?

> Don't become so well-adjusted to your culture that you fit into it without even thinking. Instead, fix your attention on God. You'll be changed from the inside out. Readily recognize what he wants from you, and quickly respond to it. Unlike the culture around you, always dragging you down to its level of immaturity, God brings the best out of you, develops well-formed maturity in you. (Romans 12:2, *The Message*)

Are you becoming so well adjusted to your culture that you fit into it without thinking? If this is the case, I can guarantee that you are pleasing your mates over God, and you are probably one person in your youth group on a Sunday morning and someone completely different, possibly ungodly, before your mates. You are doing everything that your friends want you to do so that you will fit in, gain approval and be liked. The culture around you is dragging you down. Stop! Think, right now, about the things that do not please God. It is time for us to turn our focus from our mates, fix our eyes on God and start to please him.

We all suffer from peer pressure in one way or another. I love chick flicks, especially *Never Been Kissed*. Josie Gellar (Drew Barrymore) finally gets her chance to write a real news story when she is assigned an undercover story in a school. As a teenager, Josie was a typical school nerd, and as a reporter she still can't fit in with the cool kids. We get to the end of the film and Josie saves a nerdy girl from having dog food chucked all over her, and the cool kids turn on her. Josie is tired of their self-important attitudes and decides that it is time they knew this. Josie explains that it doesn't matter whether you are Prom Queen, a football player, a cool kid or a nerd, as in the real world it is what you have on the inside that counts. She finishes with a great statement: 'Find out who you are . . . and try not to be afraid of it.'

That is what I want you to do. Don't be ruled by your mates; find out who you really are and don't be afraid of it. Are you really in the group of friends that you are in because you like their music, their particular style of clothes or the stuff they get up to? Or do you have a desire to be respected and therefore you will just put up with this stuff anyway, even lying by pretending you do like it? I know what it is like to be in this place. When I was younger I couldn't play football, but my mates could. Every day at the end of school they would be on the field or in the streets kicking a ball around. I couldn't play, but I wanted to be like them, so I bought a book on how to play football and practised and practised in my back garden – but I just couldn't do it. In the end I realised I had to be me. You see, God looks at each one of us and is pleased with what he sees; he is pleased with 'me'. God looks at you as his son and says exactly the same over you as he said over his Son Jesus: 'This is my Son, whom I love; with him I am well pleased' (Matthew 3:17).

God is well pleased with you, bro! You muck up and get things wrong; we all do, but God is still pleased with you. When you become pleased with who you are and how God has made you, you will not need to try and impress your mates, but will just be yourself. Then you will start to attract a whole new group of mates who will like you for being you. Aren't these the sort of mates you actually want? I do.

In this context, let's look at some important issues we're faced with in lad culture.

The bully or the bullied?

Do you bully lads? Do lads bully you? In my life I know that I have been in both situations. When I was younger I used to bully out of jealousy. One particular mate of mine was really good looking and all the girls used to fancy him. Girls didn't really fancy me – I was a bit spotty! I didn't like the way the girls were all over my mate, so I used to kick him. I used to kick this lad so much that he would cry, and in some really sad way this made me feel good. Out of my own jealousy I bullied this guy to make me feel that I could control him and make him feel a bit of my own unhappiness. This is a sad way to live and was very much based upon my own insecurities and how I felt about myself. Lad culture is ruled by an attitude of domination. We all like to be the 'man' and impress, whether this is with our mates, on the footy pitch, in a pub, at school or at work. We all like to get one up on the other lads, making us feel superior and respected. This is such a dangerous trap to fall into. It can be manifested both in obvious ways, such as physical bullying, and in less obvious ways, such as emotional bullying, which can take the form of having a cheap laugh at one of your mates, dissin' him and making him feel little so that you can feel big. Examine yourself and see whether you are falling into this trap.

Bro, if you are bullying others you need to start to deal with it now. The solution is to discover who you are in God. There will be some blatant issues in your life that you need to face up to, sort out and seek healing for. Check out the chapter called 'It's not about me – or is it?', which will help you on this score.

If you are the one being bullied, I have been there too. I remember running home in tears after a day of no one talking to me, lads in the classroom whispering about me and other lads physically beating me up. This is painful stuff. Some people told me to stand up for myself, and not let those bullies get me down, while others told me to put my head down and get on with it. I tried to listen to all these different voices and they just got me in a mess! I wish there was a simple, quick-fix solution that I could give you to help you out, but there isn't. However, I would like to make a few suggestions. Get into God. Spend time with him. Tell him about the bullying, and he will be your refuge and strength when the going gets tough. The writer of Psalm 46 is aware of God's comfort during times of distress: 'God is our refuge and strength, an ever-present help in trouble.'

Jesus was bullied on many occasions and was eventually stripped, whipped and left to die on a cross – murdered, the ultimate form of bullying. If you haven't realised that, watch Mel Gibson's film *The Passion of the Christ*. He knows exactly what you are going through, to the max! Jesus responded to the way he was bullied in two different ways. There were times when the Pharisees questioned his motives and actions, seeking to bring him down in front of the crowds. On these occasions Jesus spoke out against them, for all to hear. He even called them a 'brood of vipers'! However, when Jesus was brought before Pilate as they attempted to justify his crucifixion, he was asked whether the charges against him were true: 'But Jesus still made no reply, and Pilate was amazed' (Mark 15:5).

Jesus was accused of many things and yet often he remained silent. I know that when I was being bullied, if I had put those bullies down in front of everyone, as Jesus did the Pharisees, this may have caused more trouble than I really wanted. For the majority of the time I chose Jesus' second option, to shut up. Sometimes neither of these reactions will be right, whether we speak up, which takes boldness, or shut up, which also takes boldness. The key is that we need to get into the presence of God. When you spend time with him, just like Jesus did, God will give you wisdom on what you should and should not say. As we hear God and respond, we will dramatically change the situation we are in, because God will turn it around. If you are being bullied and want to know what to do, let me encourage you to spend time praying. Read Luke 6:26–31 and ask God to give you clarity on your actions. The situation will be turned around.

Choices

Bro, please do not make choices because of your mates. Don't pick any A-level course because your mates are doing the same; don't leave school because they are; don't get a particular job or pick a university or a college course because your mates are going there or doing the same course. And please, please, don't sleep around with girls just because your mates are! You are at a crucial point in your life where the decisions you make will be eternal. You will not be able to go back and retrace your steps. Once you have done your A-levels, they are done; once you have slept with your girl, that's it; once you have got that job, it shows on your CV. Bro, you need to be making decisions and choices purely because God is guiding you. God has a plan for your life. He told Jeremiah that he had one for him, and my guess is that if he had one for old Jez, he has one for us: ' "For I know the plans I have for you," declares the LORD' (Jeremiah 29:11).

If God has plans for your life, he is not going to keep

them to himself and not bother to let you know! So, how do we discover what choices God wants us to make? Here is an idea – ask him! As a kid I wanted to be a TV presenter, so I went for it. I worked hard, spent lots of money on it and worked day and night to become the 'next big thing'. After two years of loving the pursuit of a celebrity lifestyle, I decided to talk to God about it all. He told me to give it up and let it go; it wasn't his plan for my life. I only bothered talking to God about my choice after two whole years of working towards it. Foolish! As you make important decisions that will affect the rest of your life, bring God into it now. Pray and ask God to guide you. Make sure you continue reading the Bible, and do it daily, and God will reveal to you his plans for your life, guaranteed: 'Your word is a lamp to my feet and a light for my path' (Psalm 119:105).

Finally, as you start to make important decisions in your life, remember to talk to godly men and women around you. God brings people into our lives for a purpose, and we are encouraged to ask their advice: 'Plans fail for lack of counsel, but with many advisers they succeed' (Proverbs 15:22). Dude, don't be too proud or arrogant to ask; I have been there, and it isn't a great way to live. If you ask the advice of those around you (this could be your parents, youth leader or older people in the church), then your plans and choices will stand a better chance of succeeding.

Fashion and media

We should look our best for God as we represent him. I don't mean that you have to spend heaps on clothes, trainers and haircuts, but it's just great to see lads who have taken time over their appearance. I think that as Christians we should try to look our best as we honour God in all we do. I don't have a problem with varieties of images or styles, because they are all from God. Image and variety are both part of the nature of God: 'Then God said, "Let us make humankind in our image, in our likeness"' (Genesis 1:26). God is a God of infinite variety, infinite taste, styles and cultures, and therefore whatever particular culture you come from, it expresses the variety of God. However, we should not be ruled by fashion and we should not be ruled by the 'blokey' images we see in the media.

When I was younger, the peer pressure of my mates and the media affected me big time. I wanted to be a cool kid, liked and respected by the lads around me, so I tried to be what I wasn't. I wanted to gain a muscly body as I thought this was a quick-fix solution to being liked. It wasn't. I spent one summer working out with some weights almost every day, and it became an addiction. Because of media bombardment I had got it into my head that if I was muscly my friends would respect me more and the girls would come flocking – they didn't. I tried to be what I wasn't because I was ruled by the media images of how a lad should look. Don't fall into this trap. Be yourself. It isn't wrong to want to have the right clothes, to get a bit sportier, become athletic or even go to the gym. Your motives are the important part. Are you trying to impress your mates or please God? The Bible tells us to honour God with our bodies (1 Corinthians 6:20), and if this is our motivation then it is fine to play sport, go to the gym, have a nice haircut and get some new clothes. But if your motivation is to impress your mates, gain more friends and have the girls come running, sort yourself out – this isn't godly!

Clubbin'

Dude, don't follow your mates who go to clubs to 'pull', 'get laid' and take a girl home – this is wrong and you know it isn't what a rad lad is all about. Nightclubs are a fantastic way to worship God. You can worship God on the dance floor; there are heaps of secular songs with lyrics that can be used to glorify God. It's great! I know it isn't easy, when the alcohol is flowing, there are girls walking round looking hot, the atmosphere kicks in and after a few drinks you get it into your head that it would do you the world of good to kiss a girl and even take her back to your place. Don't! First, if you are going to a nightclub, make sure that you take a Christian mate with you. Ask him to keep an eye on you and allow him to pull you back on the dance floor if you start to get too fresh with a girl. Second, before you go to the nightclub make sure that you pray with your mate, asking for God's protection, wisdom and inspiration to help you worship. God wants to be included in every part of your lifestyle, including on the dance floor. Finally, keep an eye on your alcohol intake. Don't drink too much. Beyond a certain point, you won't enjoy it anyway.

Beer and smoking

OK, it's not unnatural to like a bit of alcohol. However, in your quest to be a rad lad it is important that you are godly in this area of your life too. Whether you are allowed to drink alcohol or not is dependent upon your age and whose house you are in. You should not be buying alcohol if you are under 18; this is the law and God tells us to stick to it:

> Everyone must submit himself to the governing authorities, for there is no authority except that which God has established. The authorities that exist have been established by God. Consequently, he who rebels against the authority is rebelling against what God has instituted, and those who do so will bring judgment on themselves. (Romans 13:1)

God wants us to honour the laws of the land unless they are ungodly. If you disobey the law, you are rebelling against God and this will inevitably lead to further ungodly action, whether this is getting in a fight, losing control of yourself, or getting up to things with girls that you shouldn't. It isn't wise! So if you are in a pub and you are under 18, don't buy alcohol; if you are in a shop and you are under 18, don't buy alcohol. If your mates are buying alcohol to drink at home, in the park or on some street corner, it doesn't matter that they may have broken the law and you haven't. Just don't drink it. Seek to honour God in all that you do, rather than try to impress your mates!

So you are over 18, and drinking alcohol is not wrong or ungodly. Jesus drank it and even turned water into wine. However, the concern comes if we start to drink beyond our limit. God wants to be in control of our lives, but when we drink too much the alcohol starts to take control and we make wrong decisions. When you are in a nightclub, a pub or with your mates, don't allow them to encourage you to go beyond your limit. Know your limit and stop one or two drinks before it – now that's rad lad livin'! Honour God in this and I guarantee that he will bless you. No more nights of getting into bed with a spinning head, promising God that this is your last time. Stick to the limit that God gives you! Your mates will see God in you, they will start to take note, and you will slowly see a change in their lives.

Smoking wrecks your body. Over 120,000 smokers die per year; 450 children start smoking every day. The effects of smoking range from back pain, depression, asthma and a low sperm count to various cancers. About one fifth of Britain's 15-year-olds (19% of boys) are regular smokers – despite the fact that it is illegal to sell cigarettes to children aged under 16 (www.ash.org.uk). The Bible says that we should offer our bodies to God (Romans 12:1). God doesn't want what is unclean and he doesn't want to see your body harmed through neglect. Dude, if you smoke, my guess is that you want to, and now it is time to do something about it. Get help and stop.

Changing lad culture

As we gain an understanding of what God thinks of us, we choose, out of our love for God, to please him by our actions. Quite simply, God and not our mates begins to rule us. Suddenly, something significant starts to happen, and you realise that you are no longer ruled by the culture that you are in. Instead, you start to change it. I am not saying that you should give up all your mates, run to the church and be a 'nice' boy. What a stupid idea, and what an easy way out of the real world! What I am saying is that if we begin to appreciate that God is pleased with us, and out of a love for him start pleasing him with our actions, we grapple with these issues that are part of lad culture and no longer act as followers but as leaders. The way we refuse to give in to peer pressure will stand out; our mates will respect us and they will start to follow our godly actions. Suddenly you start to become Jesus to your mates and seriously impact your group of friends, turning lad culture on its head. Sorted! Let's do it!

Sort it out

Think about whether your actions are ruled by your mates. If they are, why is this? Be honest about your insecurities and needs. Be real with yourself. In what areas of lad culture life are you not honouring God? List them, then bring your list before God and check out what the Bible says about each of these areas. Have you been bullied? The Bible encourages us to forgive those who do wrong against us; we must forgive those who bully us. Take this to God and ask him to help you forgive. Pray and ask God to help you change in these areas, and think about how you can start making small steps to see that change take place.

Big bruva

Share your list with your big bruva. Tell him honestly what areas of lad culture you are struggling with and ask him to help you see how to change. If you feel that you are addicted to alcohol or smoking, talk to your big bruva and ask him to help you. Dude, some of your mates won't be up for the rad lad decisions that you make, and it won't be easy. Talk to your big bruva, tell him how you feel and how your mates are reacting; ask him to give you advice and to pray you through the way those around you may react to your godly decisions.

Respect to rad lad

Monday mornings, and the sixth-form common room would be alive with weekend gossip – stories of drunken exploits, Saturday night punch-ups and sexual encounters would filter down the corridors. Each week someone would become a hero in the sight of the entire sixth form.

It was at the weekend that you could earn respect to make that transition across the common room. If your weekend adventure was worthy, you could move from the social outcasts' area to the side of the room where the coolio people sat.

I was desperate to migrate. I wanted people to see Andy Frost as a real lad – as a confidently cool person who demanded respect. So I decided to compromise my faith and find acceptance from fellow sixth-formers by adopting their lifestyle.

The biggest issue that hindered my transition was a real lack of self-confidence. I still stuttered occasionally, and being known as a vicar's kid did not help! With a desire for my 15 minutes of fame, I needed a new confidence and in beer I thought I had found it. I began to drink heavily each weekend and as my falsely induced confidence grew, I would make the headlines with ungodly behaviour.

The transition began, but I soon discovered that people did not like me for who I was but for what I did. Each weekend I would be dared to drink more, to do more outrageous things, and my weekends became pressurised as I tried to earn respect.

At 18, I worked on a Christian summer camp and it was at this time that I began to find a real confidence – not in drink or impressing people, but in Christ. I began to discover that when I stepped out of my comfort zone for him, I gained a supernatural confidence that took away my stutter and gained me respect in a whole different way.

As I continue on with God, seeking his will for my life, I have found true confidence rather than the masquerade that beer gave me. As I daily find my acceptance in him, I have found that when you really let God take your life and live for him, people really do respect you. Even guys who don't share my faith respect me as I find my acceptance in Jesus and live a radical life for him.

Andy Frost, Share Jesus International
www.sharejesusinternational.com

5
wazzzup, bro?

It's been a long week, heaps to do and never enough hours to get the job done. Forget all that, it's Friday! At home I get a call from one of my best mates asking me whether I want to go to the pub with him. Within minutes I am there. We spend the whole night chilling and chatting about work, about what's going on in the world. Comedy and lad banter are mixed with dreaming sessions about the future of our lives, and of how we want to make our lives count. The night can't go on for ever and the bar staff at our local finally manage to get us out. I say goodbye to T.J., really chuffed that we have spent the evening chilling together. I get back home and a text comes through, 'GR8 to spend the evening with you mate. I love you. T.J.' I lie in bed thinking how incredible it is to know what your mates think about you, to know that you are loved, cared for and appreciated. Wicked!

I am in hot pursuit of authentic lad friendships; friendships that mean something and have a great depth of worth and value about them. As we live out our lad friendships as God intended, they will have a role to play in transforming society and lad culture in a big way. When I was younger I was desperate for a mate who would be my buddy, someone I could hang out with and reveal my problems to. I was desperate for a mate who would just be there for me and I for him. I continue to develop these friendships and to live out this authentic style of friendship. Have you ever watched Ant and Dec? Those guys are hilarious. They hang around together, they are there for each other, they banter with each other and they seem to care genuinely about one another. In 2001, their friendship was recognised so much that they were named the UK's 'best mates' (www.ananova.com). I am after lad friendships that would be recognised and awarded in this same way, aren't you?

Bro, we have got the way we live out our lad friendships completely wrong. God is gutted. We need to be honest with ourselves. Society, not the Bible, has ruled the way we love, care and show affection towards the lads around us. The truth is, we are fundamentally desperate to know that the mates we hang out with love us. I use the word 'love' deliberately! We also need our mates to know that we have this same love and appreciation for them. I certainly need to know this in my own life. We ask our mates how they are, but do we hang around for an answer? We hug a mate on the footy pitch when he has just scored a goal, but off the pitch we can't show how we truly feel. If we think that a girl likes us, we will do anything to show her appreciation – bringing her gifts, spending time with her, doing things that will please her. When it comes to the lads, we live surface-level friendships and fail to talk about how we truly feel. Surely we have got something wrong.

A generation of 'Friends'

I love to watch *Friends* – it rocks! Joey and Chandler are
certainly trying to figure out a deeper lad friendship. After
being flatmates for a number of years, Joey and Chandler
have a deep bond through investing in each other in a
personal and emotional way. We get to episode 216 and the
two friends have an argument. Joey is moving out. Their
argument is a typical blokey, surface-level argument that
hides their actual pain, the fact that they love each other and
are going to miss each other big time! Eventually everyone
helps Joey carry his stuff downstairs, and Joey and Chandler
are left in the flat. They don't know how to part properly,
and after some hesitation and an awkward silence, one
simply mutters, 'Bye, see you at the café,' and Joey leaves.
Chandler is left standing devastated and lonely until Joey
throws the door open, runs in and gives Chandler a big hug.

We all have this God-given need to love and be loved, but
we avoid showing it because in today's society any affection
we show towards a bloke – a hug, telling a mate you love
him, or asking whether you could spend some time together
– would result in us fearing that those around us may think
we are gay. As Christian lads we have become fearful of man
and of what society says we should and shouldn't do, instead
of fulfilling some important biblical commands. This has to
change and someone has to take the first step.

Bro, society rules the way you should behave and
show affection towards your mates. You may live out shal-
low, meaningless male friendships, yearning to go deeper
in a way that would revolutionise lad culture and put a stop
to society ruling how we 'should' be. Lad friendships are
in desperate need of change, and it is us rad lads who

are going to make that change! Deal?

Jonathan and David – a rad lad friendship

The friendship of Jonathan and David, in the book of Samuel, is an Old Testament example of how God wants us to live out lad friendships. Check it out in 1 Samuel 18:

> By the time David had finished reporting to Saul, Jonathan was deeply impressed with David – an immediate bond was forged between them. He became totally committed to David. From that point on he would be David's number-one advocate and friend. (1 Samuel 18:1, *The Message*)

Amazing stuff! Have you ever had a mate you have just connected with? They are real, they make you laugh and they are there for you. This is what Jonathan saw in David, and a lifetime's friendship was formed. The words used to speak of his love for David are strong. Wouldn't you like a mate who is 'totally committed' to you? Someone who becomes your 'number-one' friend?

I have told you about T.J., a close friend to me and Vikki. I remember the first day I met T.J. He was watching a band play in the centre of town, and as he was watching, I watched him. I saw something in T.J., something real special. I could see in him both a strong leader and a vulnerable person, someone who craved friendships and was passionate for the heart of God. Just like in the story of Jonathan and David, when I saw T.J., a bond was formed and I walked away telling Vikki that T.J. was someone I really wanted to get to know. T.J. is now very special to me, I love him to bits and he is my number-one friend. I love our deep friendship and I am totally committed to him – and I seek to develop friendships with my other mates in the same way.

Get real about loving one another

Just before Jesus' crucifixion he gave his disciples an important new instruction: 'A new command I give you: Love one another. As I have loved you, so you must love one another' (John 13:34).

The Greek word for that 'love' is *agape*. *Agape* is the spiritual and selfless love that Jesus modelled for humanity. We are called to love our mates in the same way. The disciples were pointed to God through the parables that Jesus told, but it was his actions that highlighted the deep and selfless love he had. Dude, this is a biblical command that we have completely fallen short of. If we think of the lifestyle of Jesus, how he loved and served even to the point of death on a cross, and if we are commanded to love our mates in the same way – man, are we failing!

An *agape* love for our mates means that in everything we do we point them to God, by encouraging them in their walk and leading by example in the way we love and serve. The radical friendship of Jonathan and David shows us how this love should be. After Jonathan had developed his bond with David, something quite special happened. Out of an overflow of his love for David, Jonathan wanted to serve him: 'Jonathan said, "Tell me what you have in mind. I'll do anything for you"' (1 Samuel 20:4, *The Message*).

Out of an overflow of God's love, he sent his Son to die on the cross: 'For God so loved the world that he gave his one and only Son . . .' (John 3:16). Out of Jonathan's love for David, he exclaims, 'I'll do anything for you.' Do you have mates who will do anything for you? Will you do anything for your mates? Vikki and I both have authentic friendships across the country – mates we would do anything for. We have told them that if they are in need they should call us, knock at the door or send a text, any time, day or night. It is out of an overflow of our love for our mates that we will do anything for them, and it amazes me daily to know that I have mates who will do exactly the same for me.

We need to get real about loving our mates and progress towards rad lad friendships. I want to encourage you to show them an *agape* love, a real love that is completely self-less and points your mates to God. I believe that as lads we need to make steps forward with our friendships in four main areas: radical expression, radical servanthood, radical fellowship and radical grace.

Radical expression

> One of the disciples, the one Jesus loved dearly, was reclining against him, his head on his shoulder. (John 13:23, *The Message*)

What an image! As Jesus chilled with the disciples, the particular disciple Jesus loved had his head on his shoulder. Neither Jesus nor this disciple lived in fear of being branded gay. Why is it that we can give a lad a hug on the football pitch but we don't feel we can show any physical expression of our love off the pitch? Recently I was having a tough time and had spent some time talking to T.J. about this. We had talked previously about how as lads we should show affection towards each other, and not just the 'pat on the back with a blokey grunt' type of hug – you know the one! T.J. was about to leave, when he stopped and said, 'Give me a hug.' I was well surprised when he grabbed me and hugged me in a way that meant something. It was a great hug at the right time. When you see a mate of yours, give them an expression of your love that is relevant to where you are at in terms of your friendship. For some, the next step is to hug them, for others it is to move beyond a blokey hug, for some it will simply be to say, 'Cheers for being a mate.' However you express your love, I can guarantee that your mate will be truly blown away and your friendship will take that step further into being a rad lad, godly friendship.

We also need to express our love radically through tokens of appreciation. We've all bought gifts for a girl, but have you ever bought a gift for a lad? I have a mate who has been helping his best mate through a real tough time. This lad had saved up some money to express his thanks, and turned up at my mate's door one day with a present – the latest games console that he had wanted for ages. My friend was blown away! He had given his time, energy, care and friendship, and his best mate wanted to give him a gift to say 'thank you'. You needn't be that excessive, but have you ever thought of saving some money and buying your mate the latest CD he is after, or buying his lunch for him as a small thanks? The gift doesn't have to be big, and we don't have to make a song and dance about giving it – it could simply be a pint at the pub. What I am saying is that if we really do love our mates, then let's just start showing that by offering them a radical expression of our love without expecting the same in return – otherwise it isn't *agape* and it isn't rad!

Radical servanthood

I am married to Vikki, who is beautiful. Quite often I tell her I love her, but I have learnt something really important. If I don't back up my words with action, then what I say is meaningless. If God said he loved the world but didn't follow through by allowing his Son to die, we would never enter into relationship with him and his claim would be mere words. Jesus loved the disciples – he invited them into his life and turned them into rad lads who would ultimately change the world. Jesus expressed his love through the way he served them, even washing their smelly feet! Jesus has called us to do the same for our mates, to follow his example by radically serving our friends.

> When he had finished washing their feet, he put on his clothes and returned to his place. 'Do you understand what I have done for you?' he asked them. 'You call me "Teacher" and "Lord", and rightly so, for that is what I am. Now that I, your Lord and Teacher, have washed your feet, you also should wash one another's feet. I have set you an example that you should do as I have done for you.' (John 13:12–15)

The disciples would have worn open-toe sandals and walked for miles, so their feet would have been really sweaty and smelly. In cleaning their dirty feet, Jesus modelled an extreme example of servanthood. Serving people means doing things that you may not necessarily want to. Jesus told the disciples that they should wash one another's feet, after the example that he had shown. Jesus is not saying we should wash the feet of every mate we meet, but we should serve our mates in the same way he served his mates, with an *agape*, selfless love that mirrors the love of God. How do you serve your friends? Have you ever asked a mate whether there is anything you can do for them, just like Jonathan and David? Despite what we feel, what we are going through and how much of a sacrifice something may be, it is essential, if we are going to be rad lads, that we start serving our mates in this way. Be open with them, tell them that you are there for them, that you are prepared to do anything, and that if they need your time, to chat or to pray, then you will be ready. It is now very common for our mates to come into our house, open our fridge and help themselves without having to ask, or put the kettle on and offer us a drink! Once you start letting your mates know that you are available, they will start coming to you and you will find a greater depth of relationship as you go all out to serve them in the same way that Jesus served his best mates. Go for it!

Radical fellowship

I am after community in my own life; whatever is mine is God's anyway, and it is his to be used to bless others. Fellowship was at the heart of the church that was established in Acts:

> They devoted themselves to the apostles' teaching and to the fellowship, to the breaking of bread and to prayer. Everyone was filled with awe, and many wonders and miraculous signs were done by the apostles. All the believers were together and had everything in common. Selling their possessions and goods, they gave to anyone as he had need. Every day they continued to meet together in the temple courts. They broke bread in

their homes and ate together with glad and sincere hearts, prais-
ing God and enjoying the favour of all the people. And the
Lord added to their number daily those who were being saved.
(Acts 2:42–47)

We need to be around each other in the same way that the
early church was. Grabbing time together cultivates deep
friendships that affect the communities we live in and really
shows them what God is all about. Let's break this down.

The rad lads in Acts made sure they got time together.
Get your mates, go out and have fun, go bowling, go to the
pub, go laser questing, get into one another's homes and
talk to each other. Ask each other how you are doing and
then pray together. Fellowship is about letting lads into your
lives and into your heads, and getting into theirs in order to
help them out. Lads aren't very good at expressing how they
feel or what is going on in their lives, and therefore we have
to ask questions. I am always saying to my mates, 'Tell me
what you're thinking.' When they do, I start to get a true
glimpse of how my mates are feeling, what they are going
through and what they need help with in their lives. Then I
go further: 'How is your relationship with God?' 'How is
your prayer and Bible reading?' 'How are you dealing with
lust?' All these questions and their answers are essential if we
are going to become rad mates.

The disciples had food together, they prayed together,
worshipped together and looked at the Scriptures together.
Have you ever done this? It's good! It isn't some cheesy
Bible study, but when you really get to hear what's going on
in the lives of your mates and you spend time talking and
praying over it, God completely blesses you:

> How good and pleasant it is when brothers live together in unity . . . For there the LORD bestows his blessing, even life for evermore. (Psalm 133:1–3)

There is a real intimacy about being with my mates, and I want to encourage you to spend more time with the rad lads around you in this way too. In Acts, when the early church chilled together and ate together, then their love for each other inevitably deepened, and consequently everything that was theirs was available to each other. This is a great place to be in. I love giving to my mates. I love it when they come in and help themselves to our fridge, because our friendship has then gone past surface level. I love it when a mate can call me and not feel embarrassed about asking for some money, because there is real depth in that relationship. It's great to have 'everything in common', and it is incredible to be on the receiving end of this too: from our mates I have received money, cars, food and clothes, because out of the depth of love they have for me, they want to give to me.

Radical grace

Let's go back to the disciples. Jesus is washing their feet, just before he is about to be betrayed, handed over and crucified. Who betrays him? You don't need to 'phone a friend' or 'ask the audience' and I am not taking away two wrong answers! The disciple Judas betrays Jesus. Jesus knows exactly what Judas will do, but where is he? Yes, Judas is having his feet washed by the big guy himself! This amazes me. Jesus knows he will be betrayed by one of the lads he has invested time, love and energy into, and of course this will completely hurt him. Wouldn't you be hurt? But how does Jesus treat him?

With grace! Jesus washes Judas' feet and includes him with every other disciple.

Let's face it, we all mess up and get things wrong. When your mates mess up, do you get angry with them, or do you show them the radical grace that Jesus showed to Judas? I know that in my own lad friendships I have got things wrong and I have let people down. If my mates remained angry and upset and never forgave me, then I wouldn't have the true friends I have around me today. It certainly isn't easy, but we should seek to be radical in the grace we offer. When mates let me down I get upset and angry, because I know that I invest a lot of time and energy into these people. Sometimes I say things I shouldn't say, or I just get annoyed and walk off. Other times I feel like I could just hit them! God is teaching me to extend radical grace. If your mates let you down, take your anger and frustration to God – he can handle it! Then go to your friend and talk to him honestly and openly about how you feel, and even offer an apology for the anger you have felt towards him. If you act in this way, God will do the rest as he builds your character and begins to nurture and train you into becoming a rad friend who will change the lives of your mates.

The world's desire

As we start to live out a radical expression of servanthood, fellowship and grace, something significant will start to happen. God will add to our number; more people will become saved. This is what I am talking about, bro; this is where my heart is. When we get past the rubbish of not being able to tell our mates how we truly feel, but show them the love we have for them and share our stuff, then the world will see something. Other lads will want what we have, because deep down they have a desire for meaningful friendships too, and people will come to know God because of it – guaranteed!

Sort it out

- Take some time out and thank God for the ultimate rad lad friendship you have in Jesus. Make sure you develop and cultivate this friendship first through prayer, Bible reading and worshipping. Take time just to chill in the presence of Jesus.
- What kind of friend are you? Take a look at the four radical areas in this chapter and think about whether you offer these to your mates.
- Pray and ask God to bring a close friend to you who will invest in your life in this way too.
- Take a look at the Gospels and see how Jesus gave a selfless love to his mates. As you learn from him, seek to apply this in your own life.

Big bruva

It is not easy to give a selfless love to our mates; quite often we expect something in return. There are times when your mates have let you down. Talk to your big bruva about these occasions. How did they let you down? How did you react? Be completely radical and ask your big bruva to show you how Jesus reacted to the people around him who let him down, and start to apply that same response to your own life.

Respect to rad lad

Why does everyone else seem to have a best mate? David Beckham has Gary Neville, Ant has Dec, and even David in the Bible had Jonathan to hang out with (1 Samuel 18).

From a young age I wanted a mate I could just be myself with. I longed for someone who would encourage me and who in turn I could encourage. So I asked God for a best mate. In my case, it wasn't until I left school that eventually God answered my prayers and caused my path to cross with an old friend called Rob. That sounds all romantic, doesn't it! Rob and I used to play rugby together; in fact we used to pray together before matches. At school he was a year younger than me and so we were never really that close. After finishing school, though, it became clear that God was teaching us both about the importance of having close godly guy mates.

Everyone talks about being accountable with a friend, and yeah, we do that – telling each other how we're getting on with reading the Bible, getting that six-pack and charming the ladies, etc. – but more importantly, we're developing a real love for each other. Not in a homosexual way, just in the way that you know you'd be willing to do anything for your mate (well, steady!). Jesus even had a best mate, John, and the Bible talks about John being the disciple whom Jesus loved (John 19:26). It's so good to have a mate you can go to the gym with, ask embarrassing questions and pray with. In fact, with Rob and me, praying together every time we meet or talk on the phone has been awesome. By getting things out in the open, Satan has no hold over you and there are a lot of things I'd rather share with Rob than a girl or my parents. We can then pray more specifically for each other about these issues. I challenge Rob, try to inspire him with Scripture and ultimately long for him to get closer to God. Rob does the same for me. God has provided for me in a way I had always hoped for – he's given me a best buddy!

Christian lads have got to stick together – not in a 'God squad' way, so that we only hang out with Christians, but so that we can help equip each other for getting out there and fulfilling that call to 'make disciples of all nations' (Matthew 28:19). Don't go for it on your own: pray for a mate, pray with your mate, and together pray for all your mates. Quality!

Andy Rowlandson, student/YP writer

6
turning the tables

It's 10.00 p.m. and we are out for some time together discussing the grace of God and the challenge to be gracious in our own lives. A drunk guy decides to proclaim that the pub will be closing in ten minutes, and a lady with a small boy starts to pack away her things hurriedly. Vikki goes over to explain that the pub isn't closing in ten minutes at all, and the lady says she is glad as she is trying to figure out where she and her son can stay for the night, because her husband has thrown them out. After sympathising with this lady, Vikki comes back to me to explain the conversation and we start to throw an idea about. This lady and her child could stay at our house. A bit too radical? What if she steals our stuff? What if her husband comes to track us down and beat us up? What if they don't go early in the morning and we have to entertain them instead of getting on with our day? So many 'what ifs', but the challenge to turn the theory of grace into practice is all too clear and we invite the strangers back. Karen was blown away, humbled that we would invite them in, and Zac played the piano until all hours. Nothing stolen. No irate husband. They left relatively early the next day. We looked at Karen and Zac with compassion and God prompted that compassion to become action. We turned the tables.

Dance upon injustice

When Karen and Zac left, I began to gain a glimpse of how Jesus turned the lives of those he met upside down. Karen and Zac had been thrown out, but God didn't forget them and gave them a home for the night. As I worshipped that morning I danced upon injustice – how foolish I must have looked! Bro, it is time that we dance upon injustice. It is time to turn the tables in the world of those around us, because there are many worlds that need changing. I've told you of my bullied schooldays. If one of the Christian lads in my school had allowed God to rule them, not the crowd, the tables in my world would have been turned. What about those bullied at your college? The homeless people you walk past on the streets? Local issues of poverty or world issues of trade justice? Bro, the tables need turning and as Christians we should be the ones who start to implement change in the lives of those around us, on a local, national and international scale. A rad lad revolution of turning the tables will create a positive effect across the world. Let's dance!

Forceful man or quivering boy?

I am not talking about your age, whether you are a boy, teenager or man. I am questioning your desire for the kingdom of God. There is a great verse in Matthew, which says:

From the days of John the Baptist until now, the kingdom of

heaven has been forcefully advancing, and forceful men lay hold
of it. (Matthew 11:12)

Have you ever watched an Arnold Schwarzenegger, Tom
Cruise, Denzil Washington or Keanu Reeves film? The hero,
the action, the good guy, the force. Inspiring stuff. We want
to be like them. Dude, if we want to impact lives, see our
mates become saved, befriend the lonely, see the poor gain
much, bring healing to the hurting and truly see all that
Jesus did impact our communities once again, then we need
to see a force flow from our lives. We need a force that is
greater than anything viewed on our cinema screens; a godly
force that would positively devastate the world as we know
it. This isn't mere Hollywood stuff. It is what God is longing for, to see the Lord's Prayer finally fulfilled: 'Thy kingdom come on earth as it is in heaven.' The verse in Matthew
explains that it is those who are forceful in their advance-
ment who will truly, powerfully and effectively see the kingdom of God come. Dude, you may have stood on the
sidelines and not been forceful for the kingdom of God; you
may have been a quivering boy when it came to standing up
for peers at school, social issues or issues of injustice, or even
standing up to people older than you when you knew they
were doing something wrong. You are reading this book
because you want to be a rad lad – you want to change from
a quivering boy to a forceful man. Start now. Some stuff
needs to stop. My guess is that we have tried our evangelis-
tic events, we have put up the posters, told our mates and
tried to convince ourselves that we have put some effort into
sharing our faith. The effect? Little. We can place seeds in
people's lives that will grow and one day bear fruit, but I am
sick of us using this as an excuse for the fact that we have

pumped money, time, effort and energy into events, crusades and outreaches with little effect, all because, hands up, we weren't forceful enough. Forceful? 'But Jesus wasn't forceful!' Rubbish. Of course he was.

A stamp of approval from heaven

Remember when you were younger and you used to fight with your brother, sister or mates? They had the toy you wanted, the red pen you so desperately wanted to colour in with, or the teddy you wanted to fall asleep with. Your parents heard the commotion and pulled you off your little sibling or friend, shocked that you would use such force. But force can sometimes be used to do good – to rescue a person in danger perhaps or bring about a victory in sport. In those situations your parents may well be cheering you on. God gave Jesus the stamp of approval from heaven to be a forceful man. Jesus opened the scrolls from the prophet Isaiah and with a loud and triumphant voice declared:

> The Spirit of the Lord is on me,
>   because he has anointed me
>   to preach good news to the poor.
> He has sent me to proclaim freedom for the prisoners
>   and recovery of sight for the blind,
>   to release the oppressed,
>   to proclaim the year of the Lord's favour. (Luke 4:18–19)

God placed his Spirit on Jesus, anointed him and sent him to be forceful for the kingdom of God. Understand that you can't preach good news, proclaim freedom or release the oppressed without being forceful, and there is such a thing as godly force. If we are going to live out the command to walk like Jesus walked (1 John 2:6), then we need to recognise that we have the approval from heaven to move with a godly force in order to see the kingdom of God advance.

Passionately flipped

They must have thought that Jesus had completely lost it. You can see the men in white coats running with a strait-jacket, ready to lock him away! Check out the scene:

> When it was almost time for the Jewish Passover, Jesus went up to Jerusalem. In the temple courts he found men selling cattle, sheep and doves, and others sitting at tables exchanging money. So he made a whip out of cords, and drove all from the temple area, both sheep and cattle; he scattered the coins of the money-changers and overturned their tables. To those who sold doves he said, 'Get these out of here! How dare you turn my Father's house into a market!' (John 2:13–16)

Jesus deliberately thought through plans to make a whip; he may even have gone away and made it. This was a controlled and deliberate action used to clear his Father's house of sin. Jesus displayed his anger and displeasure with action and burning emotion – he was forceful! Passover is the celebration of God's deliverance of the Israelites from the bondage of Egypt. God's people came to the temple in Jerusalem from all over to remember and celebrate God's powerful grace. For this celebration to be used as a money-making opportunity was a violation of the feast and the temple. Jesus used the force that his Father approved of to be protective over the work and kingdom of God. Jesus was passionate about his Father's work. Bro, we need to learn to flip passionately for the kingdom of God. We need to love everything that our Father's heart is about, so much so that we defend it with godly force. The founder of World Vision made a great statement: 'If anyone wants to be a man or a woman of God they should find out what breaks God's heart and keep asking God to break their heart with the same passion.' When you are broken before God, the heart of God rules and you naturally stand up for the kingdom of God, unconcerned about what your mates think. I seriously want to be at that place. Don't you?

David the psalmist proclaims to God his passion for God's laws to be lived out in his life: 'My soul is consumed with longing for your laws at all times' (Psalm 119:20). Consumed means to be destroyed. Longing means a strong, persistent desire. So let's check this out again: 'My soul is destroyed with a strong, persistent desire for your laws at all times.' Wow! The New Testament equivalent must be Matthew 6:33: 'Seek [meaning to endeavour to obtain or reach] first the kingdom of God and his righteousness.' Get it? When you are after all that God is after, nothing will get in your way. Using force which has the approval of heaven destroys all the barriers that stand in your way. Without force the job won't get done, and without the motives of the kingdom of God you are a hindrance to God.

It's got to be godly!

I remember a retreat we ran for a group of young people who had come from across the country in order to be inspired and equipped. Weekends away of this variety are great – getting into God, worship and lots of fun until all hours. Only one problem. At that stage of my life, I was not that good or godly to be around when I was tired! On one particular night we had all had fun, it was late and we had finally got to bed. I was feeling tired and constant talking wasn't helping me gain my much-needed sleep. It was past 2.00 a.m. and one particular friend of mine was not in bed. As I was overseeing the group, I was concerned. However, my concern was expressed in anger as I jumped out of bed shouting, 'Where's Bentley? I'm going to kill him!' and charged out the room, slamming the door to a heap of laughter from the other lads. I went downstairs to the piano, where I knew this guy would be, to see him alone in a room with two girls. Two girls and one lad: not a rad lad situation, and I told him so with a few choice words. This good friend of mine who had come on our retreat received the full force of my anger, and it was certainly not godly anger!

In order to be forceful, we have to get angry, but our anger is only godly when we are operating in love. 'Love is patient, love is kind. It . . . rejoices with the truth' (1 Corinthians 13). I certainly wasn't showing love to my friend; I was showing ungodly anger. The Greek philosopher Aristotle rightly wrote, 'It is easy to fly into a passion – anybody can do that – but to be angry with the right person at the right time and with the right object in the right way – that is not easy, and it is not everyone who can do it!' Bro, this is not easy, but this doesn't mean that we shouldn't be trying and it certainly doesn't mean that we should avoid working in a godly anger for the kingdom of God through fear of getting it wrong.

Jesus often got angry and as a result had to use force. Mark gives us a classic example:

> Another time he went into the synagogue, and a man with a shrivelled hand was there. Some of them were looking for a reason to accuse Jesus, so they watched him closely to see if he would heal him on the Sabbath. Jesus said to the man with the shrivelled hand, 'Stand up in front of everyone.' Then Jesus asked them, 'Which is lawful on the Sabbath: to do good or to do evil, to save life or to kill?' But they remained silent. He looked round at them in anger and, deeply distressed at their stubborn hearts, said to the man, 'Stretch out your hand.' He stretched it out, and his hand was completely restored. Then the Pharisees went out and began to plot with the Herodians how they might kill Jesus. (Mark 3:1–6)

Jesus got angry, with the right people, at the right time, with the right objective. Nice one! Jesus was able to get angry in this way and use godly force because he knew the heart of God. When we don't know the heart of God and are not living out the character traits of Jesus, we are not operating in godly anger. Paul tells us in Ephesians: 'In your anger do not sin' (Ephesians 4:26).

Out of my anger, I sinned. I was not being loving or compassionate towards my friend. I was operating out of ungodly anger, which showed itself with an ungodly force! Bro, get angry for the kingdom of God and let your anger burn and manifest in godly force that will bring about godly change as you seek the kingdom of God first. But in your anger do not sin, as this will have a more destructive effect than building up the kingdom, and lives will be damaged rather than worlds turned upside down.

The result is?

We have the ability to use godly force, combined with godly

anger, in order to turn the tables upside down in the lives of those around us. Have you seen the film *Schindler's List*? Oskar Schindler sees an opportunity to make money during the Second World War. He owns a factory in Poland and uses cheap Jewish labourers from the concentration camps to keep it running. Over time Schindler develops compassion for his workers and requests more Jews from the camps in order to save them. By the time Germany falls, he has lost his fortune but spared 1,100 Jews from the gas chambers. At the end of the film, Schindler walks to his car where over 1,000 people are waiting to thank him for saving their lives. However, he looks at his clothes, car and jewellery knowing that if he'd sold these things they would have been worth so much more than they could ever be worth in his possession. Now there is a rad lad who used force in order to turn the tables in over a thousand lives and generations to come. Our godly force and anger may change thousands of lives, or may change just one. Both results are equally favoured in the eyes of God. Doing something is better than doing nothing, as Mother Teresa pointed out in her famous radical comment: 'If you can't feed a hundred people, then feed just one.'

Vikki and I recently received a thank-you card from Karen and Zac. Karen wrote: 'I really don't know what would have happened to myself and Zac that night. I just thank God that he placed you in our path!' Karen and her husband are now going to counselling. God used us to turn the tables in their lives. Bro, God wants to use you to turn tables in people's lives. Get forceful, get some godly anger and seek the kingdom of God first, above your mates, and see lives around you transformed through the way that God will use you. Let's get going!

Sort it out

- Take some time out to think about whether you are a forceful man or a quivering boy. Think about how you react in certain situations.
- Make a list of the things that you respond to with an ungodly anger – teachers, parents, work. Take this list to God and ask him to turn your anger into something that is godly.
- Ask God to break your heart with the things that break his.
- Think about a life that you could change. Perhaps a homeless guy, or someone bullied at school, or maybe you could sponsor a child.

Big bruva

There is a fine line between human anger that leads to sin and godly anger that leads to change. Talk to your big bruva about the things in your life that you respond to with an ungodly anger. Take a look in the Bible together, looking at how Jesus responded to situations with a godly anger. Make it a constant prayer together that God will help you to respond to situations his way.

Respect to rad lad

I had been travelling for a couple of days and finally arrived high up in the mountains in northern Thailand. It was misty and I could make out rows of bamboo huts dotted along the mountain edge. I was visiting a refugee camp, housing thousands of families who had fled the persecution of the Burmese military junta. Their villages had been burnt down and many who fled had been shot dead, raped, or taken as forced labour. These were the survivors.

I'll remember one of them for the rest of my life – I can picture her face now. She looked me in the eye and asked me to help. Although she was only 12, she was the eldest in her family and looked after the household. She didn't know what had happened to her dad, and her mum was ill in the camp's hospital. I was angry and upset that she and the thousands like her had suffered such horrors. How could the world allow it to happen? What could I do?

Before going on this trip, I had prayed that God would start using me to fight for the poor and for justice. A dangerous prayer, as it turned out. I had finished my degree and was wondering what to do next. I found myself working at Tearfund, a relief and development charity, speaking and writing about issues of justice and poverty.

God is a God of justice and he loves the poor. In the Bible, one in every sixteen verses concerns the poor. In the Synoptic Gospels (Matthew, Mark and Luke) it's one in every seven and in James it's one in every five. Justice is on God's agenda.

But it's not just Burma, or China, or just 'overseas'. Injustice is everywhere – down your road, across your street – and you too can get involved.

Andy Baldwin
www.tearfund.org/youth

7
porn, lust and . . .

Mom and dad are in bed thinking that their sweet and inno-
cent son is travelling off to dreamland. Yeah right! More like
Fantasy Island! For you the night has just begun as you shut
your bedroom door and lock the world out with it. Your
heart is racing and the adrenaline rushes as you hear the
whirr of your computer warming up. Who knows where
tonight will lead? Who knows what babes you will talk to or
what porn sites you will be checking out? You enter a chatroom and instantly a message pops up: 'a/s/l?' You take
your clothes off and that comforting feeling of getting
horny once again takes over. You know the rest of the story,
a cocktail of porn sites and chatting to girls – anything to get
you horny. By the end of the night, with your trousers round
your ankles, you will have reached your own ultimate climax,
but as you get into bed the guilt creeps in once again and
you fall asleep pleading with God for his forgiveness, a place
remembered many times before. You fall asleep promising
that you will never do it again. Deep down you know that
this time will not be the last, just like the many times before.

An apology

I am both annoyed and sorry that this subject is rarely commented on in our local churches. I have lost count of the number of lads I have spoken to on this issue who are wrapped up in guilt, shame and addiction, and this is partly down to the fact that the church as a body has let lads down through not talking about it. Bro, if the church has let you down, I am deeply sorry. However, the church's inability to deal with this subject is no excuse! Before you read this chapter I would like you to make sure that you have checked out the chapter called 'Not guilty!' Before you tackle the subject it is essential that you understand that no matter what lustful thoughts you entertain or what websites you check out, God just wants you to repent and move on, dealing with this issue in your life completely guilt free (Romans 8:1–2). Bro, you may know that place of repeatedly saying sorry and yet sinning again and again. It is a cycle of sin that you are enslaved in and you may have had enough; you want it to stop. Good! That's a great place to be in, so let's start from there. Stopping this form of addiction in your life isn't easy, but with God and biblical understanding you can do it. As you check out what God and the Bible say about it, make a decision in your heart to be a total rad lad in this area of your life and go all out to do something about it, because it is time that you did. I am going to – are you joining me?

The sliding scale

About 95 per cent of lads wank. For some of us it has become ingrained in our daily routine, as much as watching

TV, playing on our fave console or having a game of footy. Our levels of this form of self-indulgence can range between spending most of the day locked in the bathroom to a couple of times a week or month. As in the scenario above, it can also lead to forms of addiction and ungodly, lonely living, surfing the net for porn or chatting to a daughter of God on line about stuff that you shouldn't be! Think about it: what level of the sliding scale are you on? Be real. Are you frequently getting involved in this stuff, or is it every now and then? Whatever place you are at needs to change, but don't lie to yourself; be honest and we can develop and change from there.

Masturbation – is it a sin?

Yes it is. In my opinion, it is sinful in the eyes of God for reasons which I will explain. I have heard many famous preachers and read many popular books that contain almost convincing arguments as to why masturbation is perfectly acceptable. I, as much as any other lad, would love for these arguments to be right! I have even tried to convince myself with them too. But they are wrong. They go along the lines of, 'A bloke needs to release his sexual tension'; 'It is not like we are harming anybody; it's just me, my bed and a tissue!' I would even like to have an extremely radical outlook and say that in God's eyes it is just a 'bloke's hobby' that is harmless and fun. After all, God did look upon all that he had made and say that it was 'good'. Such self-deceiving would make it much easier for me to ignore the issue when it crops up in my own life; but it is not OK, it is wrong.

What does the Bible say?

The Bible says absolutely zero about the issue, a big fat zilch, nil, nothing at all. Cheers, God, thanks for the help! OK, so there is one debatable reference in the Old Testament – check out Genesis 38:1–10. Onan spilt his 'seed' on the ground and disobeyed Old Testament law that stated that as his brother was dead he had to sleep with his sister-in-law to continue the birth line. It is unclear whether this passage is about Onan withdrawing while having intercourse or about masturbation, and it is irrelevant to the debate! But what about Jesus? Jesus was a lad; he came to earth in human form, so surely he got the urge? You know what? He did:

> For we do not have a high priest who is unable to sympathise with our weaknesses, but we have one who has been tempted in every way, just as we are – yet was without sin. (Hebrews 4:15)

Shock. Horror. Surely not! It isn't blasphemous – it's true! If it isn't true, this verse is lying, and I am not going to be bold enough to suggest that! Even though Jesus sometimes felt the desire, he didn't follow through. He was without sin. Jesus was tempted in every single way, but did not give in to temptation. Jesus is the ultimate rad lad role model for us to live by, and therefore if Jesus didn't commit the crime then we should strive not to also. So, however much I would love the situation to be different, I believe that masturbation is wrong and the things associated with it, such as pornography and lust, are also wrong. My decision has not been made lightly, but through prayer and seeking God there are four main exhibits that I want to put to you, the jury, for cross-examination.

Exhibit A: Our body is a temple

> Do you not know that your body is a temple of the Holy Spirit,
> who is in you, whom you have received from God? You are not
> your own; you were bought at a price. Therefore honour God
> with your body. (1 Corinthians 6:19–20)

This is the real deal. The Holy Spirit is living and active
within us, and our body is home to the Holy Spirit. If we
have the Holy Spirit, a gift from God, within us then it is out
of order for us to disrespect the home in which this gift
dwells – our body. It is essential that we understand that
our body is no longer our own. The hand of God formed our
bodies and we were born into the world. As we recognise
that God exists and that he sent his Son to die on the cross
for us, we make a decision to accept Jesus into our life. At
that very split second, we also hand our bodies back to God
to be used by him for his glory and his purpose. Bro, you
need to start to understand what it means to give respect to
God by treating your body in a way that would both please
him and bring glory to his name. When we masturbate we
dwell on lustful thoughts – a sexy film star, a girl in our classroom or at work – and as soon as the mind starts to wander,
the body becomes aroused. You wouldn't dream of slipping
out of a boring sermon to run to the toilets for a quick one,
because that would be disrespectful to the church. It's the
same with your body: God has chosen to dwell in it by his
Spirit. Don't disrespect God by disrespecting your body in
this way.

Exhibit B: Pure sight

Finally, brothers, whatever is true, whatever is noble, whatever is right, whatever is pure, whatever is lovely, whatever is admirable – if anything is excellent or praiseworthy – think about such things. (Philippians 4:8)

I feel convicted at the mere thought of this verse. How can I read this verse and think that masturbation is OK? I can't! The majority of lads masturbate with a lustful thought in their mind. You are feeling horny, you relax and you fill your mind with the image of a girl or sexual scenarios that you would like to get yourself involved with. It is this personal home cinema in your head that helps you 'get off' and makes your experience complete. Paul tells us to think about what is noble, pure and praiseworthy. The fantasies that I have thought about in the past, that have helped me 'get off', have certainly not been 'pure', and I can guarantee that yours have not been either!

Exhibit C: Mental adultery

You have heard that it was said, 'Do not commit adultery.' But I tell you that anyone who looks at a woman lustfully has already committed adultery with her in his heart. (Matthew 5:27–28)

OK, so you are lying in bed, you start feeling horny and you suddenly find yourself erect. You start to have all these images in your head of what you would like to do with a girl. There it is! At that point you have committed adultery with a woman in your heart, because via the image that you have in your head you are looking at her lustfully. Jesus quite clearly spoke out against adultery of any form, because it is sinful.

Exhibit D: Selfish ambition

> If you've gotten anything at all out of following Christ, if his love has made any difference in your life, if being in a community of the Spirit means anything to you, if you have a heart, if you care – then do me a favor: Agree with each other, love each other, be deep-spirited friends. Don't push your way to the front; don't sweet-talk your way to the top. Put yourself aside, and help others get ahead. Don't be obsessed with getting your own advantage. (Philippians 2:1–4, *The Message*)

How did Jesus act? He loved, he served, he put others first. That's it: his lifestyle was 'other, other, other'. Masturbation is about 'me, me, me'. Surely the fact that Christ died for our sins would be enough to compel us to put others first? Let's assess the situation. Why do I wank? Because, for that moment in time, I feel pleasure that is indescribable. As I throw myself fully and firmly into the act, the sensations drive me crazy until the whole thing is over. I do it because it makes me feel good. This verse tells us to put ourselves aside and not to be obsessed with getting our own advantage.

Here is the real deal: masturbation undermines the mutual nature of a sexual relationship and focuses on the enjoyment of ourselves, not the other person. Bro, if you continue masturbating, when you get married your focus will remain on fulfilling your own needs, not serving your wife and seeking to fulfil hers. One day, when you make love to your wife, you will have the best night ever if you seek to serve each other's needs, guaranteed. Until then, masturbating to fulfil your own desire encourages a self-centred lifestyle that we don't see in the character of Jesus – so don't do it!

Our last ray of hope?

On examination of the evidence, bro, it would seem that we are doomed. In the back of my mind I reckon I may have a last ray of hope that would enable me to continue enjoying myself in this way. What about the semen in our bodies – surely we need to get rid of it somehow? Fanfare please! Have I just saved the whole of the male species from having to deal with this issue in their lives? I have thought, prayed and sought God in this area, and I am firmly convinced that God would have designed a solution to this problem that wouldn't lead his sons to sin. I believe that God's design is the 'wet dream', or 'nocturnal emission'. This is the discharge of the semen in your body and it happens during the night. Nocturnal emission takes place when we enter a certain stage of our sleep called REM (Rapid Eye Movement). During this time there is intense activity in the brain, which means that our breathing and heartbeat can become irregular. During this stage our penis also goes erect, which eventually leads to semen being released. This doesn't lead you to websites, it doesn't lead you to talk about stuff in chatrooms that you shouldn't do, and it doesn't lead you to do anything out of selfish ambition. God is fully aware of the body that he has created and therefore he has designed it so that, at night, when we are fast asleep, our body releases these fluids and we are not led to falling into sin. God is amazing!

The final verdict

The evidence has been examined and the jury has made its decision. Four Bible passages have been put forward that strongly indicate that masturbation is wrong. The opposition came back with a defence on medical grounds, but the mighty hand of God's ingenious design has overruled. The verdict is out and the evidence is overwhelming: it is simply and categorically wrong in God's eyes for blokes to masturbate. Bro, this little obsession has taken up far too much of your time, and you know as well as I do that it is time to say goodbye to this daily ritual of yours once and for all.

In the middle of a crowd, lonely

With the increase of twenty-first-century internet connections and PCs in our bedrooms there is one situation that worries me deeply – uncensored and unlimited access to the internet. As we lock the door behind us, surf the net, chat to girls and click our way through porn sites, we are becoming one of the loneliest generations of lads ever to exist. Bro, you may have heaps of friends and be the centre of attention, or you may only have a few, but whatever the case it is loneliness that drives you to your computer and ultimately enslaves you into the addiction of masturbation. Many Christian lads are favouring cyber relationships, meaningless instant messaging or chatroom banter that fuels their desires. This isn't reality, it's not real life, and it is very sad. If this is you, stop. What you desire is deep friendships. Check out Chapter 5 to help you move into this level of friendship with lads around you.

The solution: rad lad relationships

I am going to offer you a few steps that will help you deal with the problem of porn and lust in your life. However, I believe there is only one answer that will completely resolve this situation in your life, and that answer comes through having an ultimate relationship with Jesus, who tells us: 'I have come that they may have life, and have it to the full' (John 10:10). I am convinced that we *can* know Jesus to the full, so much so that he is our every desire – an ultimate relationship with Jesus whereby we become so consumed with him that other thoughts are not enticing, because what we have in Jesus is so much more. As you seek to deal with this issue, I would like to encourage you to seek after a rad lad relationship with God, as he is the one who will enable you to become self-controlled and reduce and eventually stop this sin in your life.

Sort it out

The following are ideas that you can implement in your own life in order to protect you from falling into this sin.

● *Computer safety:* If you have a computer in your bedroom, get it out of there. Ask your parents if you can move it. If they ask why, just tell them it is too much of a distraction, and they will understand.

● *Never look twice rule:* There are images we see each day that we store in our minds. We then hit replay and use these images as fantasy fuel. If you see such images, whether this be a good-looking girl in the street, or a semi-naked girl in a newspaper or on a TV advert, the tendency is to look again. Don't!

● *Be aware of your surroundings:* If those feelings set in

and you know that you are at the 'Sack it! Any minute now I am going to find a room and fall into this temptation' stage, don't pander to your desires. As soon as you feel this, go into a room with other people – your parents, your family, a mate, a classroom – or if you are on your own get out and have a walk. Make sure that if this feeling sets in, you are not in a position where you can follow through with the act – find people!

● *Be honest with God:* 'Take captive every thought to make it obedient to Christ' (2 Corinthians 10:5). Don't dwell on lustful thoughts, but when they come into your mind pray and ask God to help you keep every thought in line with the thoughts Jesus desires you to have!

Big bruva

Be honest with your big bruva, and tell him exactly how you are doing. Ask him to pray with you and to keep checking up on you in these areas. Also ask him to help you implement ways that will stop you falling into sin.

Respect to rad lad

My story is not one of uncompromising purity, nor is it one of tangible transformation. It is, at best, a struggle to find freedom from the imprisoning chains of lust. A struggle that continues, at times with great intensity, but increasingly with periods of triumph and purity. A struggle that has been marked by repeated failure and overwhelming disappointment with my lack of self-control. On my journey I have found no formula for success, no spiritual secret, no door to a world of purity and ease. I have simply been persistent, determined, and unrelenting in seeking to live a life that pleases Jesus.

Constantly aware of my human weakness, I have pursued God in the hope that one day I will be free from the pressure of this promiscuous world and from the darkness of my own corrupted heart. I'm driven by the words of Jesus, 'Blessed are the pure in heart, for they will see God.' I will not let the momentary pleasure of sin rob me of the everlasting bliss of knowing God. Practically, this has meant that I have had to stop believing the deceiving voices in my head. My balls will not explode if I don't masturbate! If I haven't masturbated for a while I don't need to check that my plumbing is still working OK! I don't need to see if that film is suitable for the youth group! I'm learning to discern the lies that the enemy constantly feeds me. I have personally found that setting challenges for myself is also useful. I set myself a challenge not to masturbate for 365 days. After about 40 days you find that masturbation stops being habitual. The struggle continues, of course, but breaking the habit is extremely helpful. I failed after three months, but am now back up to nine months.

Don't let failure force you to give up. I'm now learning that purity is so much deeper than not masturbating; it is a new way of looking, of seeing, of understanding. I'm memorising Bible verses and trying to bring God's word alive in me. I have also found it an overwhelming encouragement to understand why God wants me to be pure. Sexual impurity does incredible damage to those it involves. By staying pure we enhance our future marriage, we protect ourselves and those who are subject to its abuse. What God asks us to do is for our good and it makes sense. God loves me and I trust his wisdom.

PS. Please don't ask me what happens after 365 days . . . I haven't thought that far yet.

James Hill, student

8
gonna do it right, girl

My girl and I are together. She is beautiful and I'm the happiest lad alive. I love being in a relationship. Sorted. Sunday afternoon, not much going on, so we chill on her bed and start to kiss and cuddle. It's great just to hold her and look into her eyes. Nice. We start getting a bit passionate and boy, do I want to go further! Slight problem, we are not married. I could convince myself that we should do it, pray for God's forgiveness afterwards and I will be guilt free. Would that please my body? Yes. Would it be honouring to God? No! We reach that point where we either go for it to please ourselves, or we stop and wait . . .

Walking a minefield

We waited! The subject of girls is a minefield – one wrong move and an explosion of hormones, emotions, guilt and condemnation could cause lifelong devastation. You may have a girlfriend or a fiancée: a nice place to be at when you are with someone who means everything to you; a bad place if you are not doing it right. All lads desire to have that girl on their arm who wants to be with them; the one we love and can share our innermost secrets with as we chill together on the sofa. No girl wants to be used and abused, though. Not one girl wants to have her boundaries pushed, be treated like a fool, used and then dumped. This isn't godly, and we fail God big time on this one! In Chapter 2 we checked out how Jesus submitted to God in all areas of his life. The subject of girls is a tough area for us blokes, but we need to submit this area of our lives to God, trusting him with our relationships. Let's go for a low-down on the major 'girl' questions we ask as Christian lads, and in doing so let's seek to make a change and be all out to honour God in the way we conduct our rad lad relationships. Agreed?

Question one: Christian or non-Christian? That is the question!

OK, so is it a problem for Christians to go out with non-Christians? As a general rule I would say yes, it is a bad idea to go out with a non-Christian girl:

> Don't become partners with those who reject God. How can you make a partnership out of right and wrong? That's not partnership; that's war. Is light best friends with dark? Does Christ go strolling with the Devil? Do trust and mistrust hold hands? (2 Corinthians 6:14–16, *The Message*)

Non-Christian girls may not understand your relationship with God, and may not be happy with you going to church, praying, reading the Bible and generally getting into God. A non-Christian girl may also not be happy with your rad lad lifestyle of not drinking alcohol, smoking or doing drugs, and she may not be happy with your 'no sex before marriage' attitude. The Bible encourages you to love God with all your heart, mind, soul and strength. A Christian girl should push you into God; a non-Christian girl may prove to be a distraction. Dude, ultimately God's concern is that a non-Christian girlfriend may pull you away from him. A life without God is a life that is lacking big time, and therefore it is not a good idea to get involved with anything that may pull you away from him!

Do you have a non-Christian girlfriend? Perhaps you may think that a non-Christian girlfriend is not a big deal. Let's question our motives. Why would we want to do something that God, who created us and who knows us better than anyone, does not think is a good idea? Answer: because of our own selfish desires! The non-Christian girl may be 'fit'; she may be the nicest girl ever to have walked this planet; it may even be impressive to have her on your arm in front of your mates. I understand that. Nevertheless, God knows you and knows what's best for you. If he does not think it's a good idea, then that's good enough for me and it should be good enough for you. If you are in this situation, you need to deal with your selfish desires, your entangled emotions, and get into God with an open and pure heart to see what he has to say, because the Dude actually does know best.

What do you mean, 'as a general rule'? Nice one! You noticed. In the introduction to this book I encouraged you to work out your own salvation before God, and you need to hear what God has to say about your relationships with girls too. I have read books and heard speakers explain that you should not go out with non-Christians, and I agree that this is a good rule – but I do think that there is an exception. The exception is when God gives you permission to go out with a non-Christian because he has a divine purpose in it. A friend of mine went out with a non-Christian because God told him to. After two years of their relationship she became a Christian. God knew this would happen and that is why he granted my friend permission to go out with her. These are unusual circumstances, but they do exist. The exception is not to be used as an excuse to go out with non-Christian girls and should only be considered in a godly context. First, is your relationship with God strong? Are you strong enough to hear God over your own emotions for this girl? Mates of mine who have experienced this are strong in God, spend time with him and are getting to know his voice over their own desires. Second, will this girl hold you back in God? If you are not mature in God, which deep down you will know, or if this girl will hold you back, then the answer is clear. Don't go out with her! Nevertheless, you should also talk your situation through with an older person, explaining the whole scenario – your feelings, thoughts, and emotions – and ask them to pray and seek God for you. Listen to their advice and respect it!

Question two: Should you go out with a girl if you have no intentions of marrying her?

A rad lad statement: if you have no intention of marrying a girl, do not go out with her. A bit harsh, you may think, and this may mean not going out with a girl until you think you have found 'the one' – even if you are aged 20 or beyond. Now you didn't want to hear that! Dude, let's be real: if you have no intention of marrying a girl, or even considering her as a potential partner, then why do you want to go out with her? The only possible reason is to fulfil your own selfish desires. Now is that really a rad lad thing to do? I can come up with two selfish reasons for wanting to go out with a girl without intentions of marriage: for physical needs and to feel secure.

Let's be honest. We love having a girl in our arms who we can kiss, touch and feel – a girl who tells us how much she loves us, cuddles up to us and wants to be near us. It makes you feel good about yourself, and you have a physical need for a girl to be dependent upon you. This need is God-given (check out the chapter entitled 'Singledom' for more details). However, the timing is completely wrong! To get physically close to a girl in this way is damaging to her and to you. Lads generally have the ability to move on, but girls get emotionally attached and to be close to her and then reject her in this way could cause years of pain and scarring that could hinder her when she eventually gets married. Imagine you had a sister who got physically close to her boyfriend, but then the relationship ended and you saw how devastated she was. You would want to go and tell the guy exactly what you thought of him! Imagine how God feels when you do the same thing to one of his daughters. We need to treat daughters of the King with respect.

It is natural to want to have a girlfriend; it gives us a sense of security. Our mates have girlfriends and we need to keep our street cred. We want to be one of the lads and we know that our mates will respect us more if we have a girl to take to parties, to take with us when we hang out and generally to show as a trophy. Bro, this is wrong. We use girls in this way like a fashion accessory, like going out and buying some new trainers: a few months down the road, they are in the bin and we are on to our next, a better model! If you are like this, it actually speaks more of your own insecurities, fear and lack of confidence than anything else, and this needs to be dealt with before you enter any relationship. The chapter called 'It's not about me – or is it?' would be a great place to start. The truth is that girls don't deserve to be treated in this way, and we should also respect ourselves more. Any girl you don't intend marrying may one day get married, and I can guarantee that when she recounts her stories of how lads messed her around both physically and emotionally, her husband isn't going to be too happy. I wouldn't be, and neither would you.

A better alternative?   We are used to the concept of 'going out' with girls. By this we mean that they belong to us, we belong to them, and we get physically intimate. At some point we need to spend quality time with a girl to discover whether she is the one we want to spend the rest of our lives with. I want to see a revival of an old-school way of getting to know a girl – dating! A dictionary definition of dating is 'an engagement to go out socially with another person, often out of romantic interest' (dictionary.com). When you go on a date with a girl, you may go bowling or for a nice walk in the park. There is no commitment or physical relationship. You are saying that you are interested and want to get to know more about each other, your likes and dislikes, in order to see whether you are compatible and whether you feel that this is a relationship God wants to take a step further. Bro, dating is the rad lad way forward.

Question three: How far is too far?

So you are in a relationship that you feel God wants you to be in. This classic question then arises. Naturally we want to go as far as we can while still feeling guilt-free and completely in a right relationship with God. Why are you even asking this question? It means that you are trying to get away with as much as possible, to fulfil the desires of the flesh rather than focusing on God. Paul has a lot to say on the subject:

> Focusing on the self is the opposite of focusing on God. Anyone completely absorbed in self ignores God, ends up thinking more about self than God. (Romans 8:7, *The Message*)

Bro, you should not be focusing on what you can be physically getting out of a girl. This is not to please her but yourself. Instead, focus on God, on loving her, treating her right and being the best example of Christ that you can be for her.

However, seeing as you asked the question: be careful where you let your hands (or hers!) go. When you are on the couch, make sure you are in a room with others. Never be behind closed doors on your own. Why? Isn't it obvious? Getting close to each other in these ways, without other people around you, can lead to temptation and sex before marriage, which is a sin. We all have various ways of being 'turned on'. For some this could be being kissed on the neck; for others this could simply be having arms wrapped around your waist. Whatever turns you on, you shouldn't be doing. Talk about your boundaries and don't cross them. In discussing boundaries, the fear is that in the heat of the moment you know exactly what will please the other, and you may use this to your own advantage! To lead a girl into sin is out of order. Bro, treat your girl with respect. It is time we were more mature in our relationships. Be the rad lad of God you are called to be. Make sure you never get to the heat of the moment stage, and if you do get there, be mature enough to walk away. God will seriously honour your rad lad livin' in this way.

Question four: Can we have sex?

I have never had sex! Not even with my wife. We make love! I am not trying to be cheesy, just honest. When I think of sex, I think of 'self'. Secular lads come back from a club with a girl and have sex. Why? Because they have a sexual desire that they want fulfilling. What about Vikki and me? Well, of course she turns me on – she's my wife! However, I want to please her sexually, and when I seek to fulfil her, and she wants to serve me in the same way, then we have a great time. This sort of intimacy is designed for marriage, not for a girl you are going out with. You may love her, you may want to be sexually pleased by her, and you may think she is the one, but making love is designed for the marital relationship. Why? Because you give a part of yourself to one another; you become one:

> For this reason a man will leave his father and mother and be united to his wife, and they will become one flesh. (Genesis 2:24)

This verse does not say leave your mum and dad and be united to a girl, go back to your parents, then on to the next girl, back to your folks again, and so on. This may be the way culture is; from sleeping around to couples who get divorced. When I was younger, my friend's dad came home to see his wife having sex with another man. Clearly his dad was devastated, and it broke the heart of my friend and his sister. We are called to honour God with our bodies. Even if you desire to marry the girl you are with, sex outside marriage can be devastating because becoming one flesh with a girl and then being ripped apart from one another is a painful thing. No daughter of God deserves to be treated like that. I love Daniel Bedingfield's song, 'Right Girl':

> I'm gonna honour your body any way I can now baby
> 'Cause we belong to somebody and that someone is G.O.D.
> When we do, we'll have wed each other
> Forsaken all others, just you and I, one another.

Instead of thinking about what *he* can get out of sex, Bedingfield thinks about making love. Instead of thinking, 'I'm feeling so horny, I want to jump into bed with you so I can be sexually fulfilled,' these lyrics are saying, 'I love you, I honour you and your body and therefore I am going to wait.' Daniel Bedingfield is a rad lad. Instead of going with the flow of society, which encourages you to sleep with your girlfriend, he shows that he is going to honour her and God and wait. If the relationship with the girl he is talking about does not work out and they haven't had sex, it will be easier for them both to cope with. If it doesn't work out, they will be glad that they didn't; if it does, then they will eventually know the mutual satisfaction of making love, and God will bless them big time.

Want a rad lad relationship?

We can be boys, fool around with girls, use them for our pleasure and then move on. This is the way of non-Christian lads and I guarantee that it will ultimately hurt you and the string of girls you leave behind. Or we can make a decision before God to be radical in the way we treat his daughters. I want to see an army of rad lads arise who will encourage their girlfriends into God, make sure they pray and worship together, and accept the challenge of growing as boyfriends who will be nothing but an example of Christ in the way they treat their girlfriends. Ultimately, even if we feel it right to end a relationship with a girl, we should be doing it in a way that honours both God and the girl we have spent our time with. Daniel Bedingfield sings, 'I'm gonna do it right, girl.' Bro, make a decision to do it right in the relationship you are in. If you are not in a relationship, decide to start growing in God in preparation for your future wife. Make a decision that when the time comes, you will do it right. This may not be what the world encourages, but it is this sort of rad lad behaviour that pleases God and impacts the world. The decision is yours!

Sort it out

- Take some time out to thank God for the gift of relationships, a wife and the ability to make love. These are all gifts!
- If you are in a relationship, write a list of the good and bad points about your relationship – what you are getting right, what you are getting wrong. Ask God to show you how to grow in getting it right and to stop what is wrong. Ask an older married couple to spend time with you, helping you through some of these issues.
- Spend time with your girlfriend, getting into God, praying together, reading the Bible and worshipping.
- As a bloke you like to be sexually fulfilled. Hand over your desires to God and make a decision to make love at the right time with the right consequences, not at the wrong time with the wrong consequences.

Big bruva

The world of relationships can be tough; we have our emotions mixed in with God's desires. Show your big bruva the list you have made about the relationship you are in and ask him to help you to be more godly in the way that you conduct your relationships. If you are going out with a non-Christian, take this to your big bruva, chat to him and pray with him in order to see what God is saying about this relationship.

We all have sexual wants and needs – sex is a God-given gift! However, the right time is vital and for me this is something that I have struggled with, having sex before marriage. The majority of relationships I was involved with before I was a Christian were handled in the wrong way and things had to change. We can start to believe that the only way we can feel love or show love is by having sex. This isn't true! As God is teaching me and moulding me into a rad lad, he is showing me better ways of expressing my love and affection to a girl. Here are a few ideas:

1. Flowers – when they say they like flowers, they mean it!
2. Going out for a meal is an excellent way of getting to know each other better without the temptations of being alone.
3. Spending time together with God, praying, worshipping and reading the Bible, will help you grow together and experience God in a new way.
4. You are the man – God wants us, as men, to take responsibility and be a leader in our relationships; not to smother and control but to see our girls grow in God.

These are a few things that have helped me, but every relationship is different. Ask God what he wants for your relationship and don't be afraid to ask other people who you look up to and respect for advice.

Live out God's way for your relationship and you can ensure that it will be strong and healthy as you grow together.

Ian Crowe, member of Soulcry
www.soulcrymusic.com

9
singledom

Don't you hate Valentine's Day? Christmas is over, 'love is in the air', and the hype encourages cute cuddly couples to gaze into each other's eyes for that split second longer. So I'm walking through town and feeling as if I'm sticking out like a sore thumb. Everyone must be watching me as they walk by hand in hand, arms around each other. What is wrong with me? Am I ugly? I haven't had a girlfriend for ages. I am lonely. As I look on, deep down I desire to have a girl, to hold and to be my own. I turn round and see a beautiful girl, long blonde hair – looks nice. She is talking to her mates, seems bubbly, lively, fun, great personality. Perhaps she is the one. I stop, stare – and see her boyfriend come out of a shop and kiss her as they walk off together. What is wrong with me? Will I be single for ever?

The lenses of youth

Do you live in the world of singledom? Big deal! I am not trying to be rude or harsh – just truthful. I was single throughout my teenage years at school and it was tough and lonely. I know what it is like. Of course I wanted a girl. Of course I wanted to be comforted, loved, appreciated, respected and all the rest. Deep down I felt that if I had a girl it would make me more of a 'man' in my own eyes and in the eyes of those around me. During those painful, lonely years I wish someone had told me the truth – that singleness is no big deal, so get on with your life. Nobody told me, so I am passing on to you what I wish I had known then. Through the lenses of youth, everything is a big deal. You build up to GCSEs and work hard (hopefully!). Don't get me wrong, these are significant exams, but then you move on to A-levels, BTEC, or a job, and this is important too. You may then go on to college or uni, and the stress and importance of the previous exams are gone as you work hard towards the next. There is more to life than this, though. Jesus died so that we may have life in all its fullness, but we are told that there is someone else out there who wants to stop us gaining this fullness of life:

> A thief is only there to steal and kill and destroy. I came so they can have real and eternal life, more and better life than they ever dreamed of. (John 10:10, *The Message*)

Bro, regain your perspective. Your hang-up about being single is robbing you of a better life than you have ever dreamed of – the life that Jesus died for. As we look at singleness, start to look at it through God's perspective, and as you do you will move further into what God has for you as a rad lad in the kingdom of God.

You're not called to be a monk!

I remember a friend of mine was not doing particularly well in getting a girlfriend and he was finding this tough. My friend then read a book called *I Kissed Dating Goodbye* (Joshua Harris). This book suggests that singleness is a better alternative to going out with a girl, until the right girl comes along at the right time. Agreed. However, my mate read this book and took it as God's personal word to him that he was to be single for the rest of his life – a twenty-first-century monk. This caused real problems a few years later when he fell in love with a girl and struggled to decide whether this was right or wrong, because he believed God had called him to be single. I have said before that being a rad lad is not about an extreme lifestyle, but more about getting into God, growing in him and figuring out where his voice is guiding you in your life over the voice of your friends, the media and the culture around you. Now that is rad lad livin'! Bro, get into God, figure out what he has for you and don't jump on the extreme bandwagon of assuming that God has called you to be single for the rest of your life. Pursue him and he will make it clear!

Coupledom verses singledom

There is no competition. No war. Society bombards us with an understanding that being one of two is the best thing that could ever happen to us. Ronan Keating sings of 'the way you make me feel', Bedingfield proclaims, 'If you're not the one then why does my soul feel glad today?', and Babyface celebrates, 'Every time I close my eyes I thank the Lord that I've got you.' Each of these artists is reflecting media-style romances: the likes of David and Victoria Beckham, Jennifer Aniston and Brad Pitt or Catherine Zeta Jones and Michael Douglas are everywhere. There is the alternative, demonstrated in films along the lines of *American Pie*. This is a story about typical teenage high school students whose aim is to have sex before they graduate – not to get a girlfriend and develop with their lifelong partner, but merely to have sex. Sex sells – not relationships, marriage, commitment and growing old together, but sex! Lad culture promotes singledom as a positive thing: if you throw off all Christian morals you can get 'laid' as many times as you want without having to be committed. Satisfaction without responsibility. But what does God say? God has blessed both marriage and singleness equally; not one more than the other, but both receiving the same blessing. Check out what Paul has to say:

> Sometimes I wish everyone were single like me – a simpler life in many ways! But celibacy is not for everyone any more than marriage is. God gives the gift of the single life to some, the gift of the married life to others. (1 Corinthians 7:7–8, *The Message*)

Bro, both marriage and singleness are gifts from God. If you are single, being single God's way is a gift. Quit looking at what your mates, the albums and the movies are saying about singleness and accept that the situation you are in at this moment is a gift from God to you.

What about what I want?

'I want!' Have you ever muttered these words to a parent, teacher, youth leader or anyone else who feels they have an ounce of authority over you, and been hit smack bang in the face with the immortal words 'I want doesn't get'? Vikki and I were engaged, it was leading up to Valentine's Day and we had the mother of all arguments – shouting, swearing, the whole shebang. We sorted it all out and I went into town to spend some time with God. I walked past shop windows crammed with Valentine's Day junk and I was telling God how I wanted to buy Vikki a significant present – something that had meaning. But we had no money. I eventually blurted out, 'God, I want to buy Vikki a pair of lovebirds!' Lovebirds live for a long time and I wanted this to be a sign of my lifelong commitment to her. God's response was certainly not, 'I want doesn't get!' He encouraged me to believe for the biggest cage for the brightest and most colourful lovebirds with a promise that he would pay for the whole lot. A few weeks later I received a cheque from a friend who explained that God had told him to give me a certain amount of money – the exact amount that I needed for the lovebird package! Vikki adored the lovebirds and cried when she received them. God rocks!

Bro, God knows that you want a relationship. We all have a need for companionship and God is certainly not saying, 'I want doesn't get!' In fact, God knows of your wants and needs because he created us to desire the companionship you crave. Let's check out Genesis:

> God said, 'It's not good for the Man to be alone; I'll make him a helper, a companion.' (Genesis 2:18, *The Message*)

God knows your 'wants' and it is OK for you to want a girl, because God created these needs in you and designed you. It is vital for you to understand that God has designed emotional, physical and sexual needs in you that will one day be fulfilled by the beautiful woman you marry. It's OK for you to feel a desire for this companionship. In God's timing your needs will be satisfied.

How the heck did Jesus cope?

No girlfriend. No kissing. No sex. How did the big guy manage? Let's take a look at the way Jesus coped with being a single guy.

Jesus watched where he looked. He certainly wasn't looking at every female he encountered wondering whether she would be his lifelong partner! Jesus was content with the gift of singleness that God had for his life, because he knew that God knew best and wanted the best for his Son. Bro, you are God's son and he wants the best for you, so be content with your singleness and watch where you look.

Jesus was in hot pursuit of a lifestyle that would please his Father God. Jesus only did what he saw his Father in heaven do (John 5:19). Jesus had to spend time in the presence of God, in prayer, worship and reading the Scriptures, in order to see what sort of living would please his Father. As a direct result, Jesus was loving, caring, compassionate and full of integrity, and he was always acting in a way that God would be well chuffed with. I want to encourage you to develop a character and lifestyle that will honour God. In doing so, you will be preparing yourself to be the very best that you can be for your future girlfriend and wife. Surely this is a great investment, so start being the best you can be for her, now!

Jesus knew he had stuff to do. Jesus knew he had one shot, one opportunity and one chance to impact the world with something he believed in. Jesus knew why he existed on this planet and he was focused on fulfilling his calling, not on the fact that he was single. In 1 Corinthians 7 Paul says, 'I wish that all men were as I am.' Paul wished that all men were single! Why? When you're married, the stuff that God has for you to do remains, but it then has to be worked out with respect to your responsibility towards your wife. I was not married when I started to walk like Jesus walked, and therefore I could devote as much time as I liked to my ministry – and to be honest I knew that it was what God wanted me to do and I loved it. However, when Vikki and I got married, for a period of time I tried to put as much work into the ministry as I had previously. This resulted in a few 'conversations' between me and Vikki. I had to recognise that I had made a binding covenant before God to put Vikki first, and therefore I had to make some adjustments to my time! I love my wife, I love being married and I would not change this for the world. Nevertheless, when you are single you have the maximum amount of time to figure out what God has got planned for you and to start living this out. Bro, use the time you have while you are single wisely and get into God and find out what he has for you to do!

Jesus was aware of his need for companionship and friendship, and therefore he pulled around him some decent mates he could spend time with. He was real, vulnerable and honest with these lads and he developed a relationship with them that would satisfy his God-given need to be in fellowship with others. Bro, you may be single, but get some decent mates around you and develop some quality relationships with them. I can guarantee that there is nothing like chilling with your mates, chatting, eating and being honest about the stuff you are finding hard, your desires for the future and the things you want to change. Go and grab time with your mates!

Jesus coped with singleness very well; in fact he probably hardly ever noticed it! Jesus was in tune with God, he knew what God had called him to do, and he had 12 of the best mates he could possibly find around him. What more could a rad lad want in order to live a rad lad lifestyle?

Cleanliness – it's what I long for!

Lads are generally renowned for not looking after themselves. If you are wondering why you are single, face up to the fact that your hygiene could be a reason! I remember when I was a teenager in Year 8: I was single and dealing with the fact that I was quite spotty. I was the sort of lad who would prefer to stay in bed until the very last minute, jump out of bed, throw some clothes on and run out the door. On numerous occasions I didn't wash my face. I remember one day, to top all this off, some lad made a joke about the fact that I had a really bad case of dandruff. I hadn't even noticed!

Let's face it: sometimes we are poor at keeping ourselves hygienic. Whether this means regular showers, deodorant, making sure we wash our face or even making sure that we get a haircut every now and then, it is essential that we deal with our cleanliness, as no girl wants to go out with a smelly boy. In Corinthians Paul informs us that the Holy Spirit lives within us and therefore we should honour God with our bodies (1 Corinthians 6:19–20). If we are truly to keep to this verse and are striving to glorify God in all we do, I believe it is essential that we make sure our personal hygiene glorifies God too. Bro, this is a sensitive subject, but I just want to encourage you to make sure you are keeping clean and hygienic, so that when the time comes girls won't be put off.

The rewards

I know that singleness isn't always easy. I have had personal experience of just how tough it can be. But God knows your situation. He created you and he knows your days from beginning to end. Proverbs says some excellent stuff – check it out:

> Trust God from the bottom of your heart; don't try to figure out everything on your own. Listen for God's voice in everything you do, everywhere you go; he's the one who will keep you on track. (Proverbs 3:5–6, *The Message*)

If we accept that singleness is a gift, thank God for this and trust him completely in it, we will be rewarded with a deeper relationship with God, and knowledge of the plans God has for our rad lad lives – plans that we can pursue. As we trust God, we will be rewarded at the right time with the perfect girl God had always planned for our lives. I remember being at school during my dandruff incident with a bad case of acne to top it all off. I was single and lonely. I wish I had trusted God. Eight years later I got married to a beautiful woman of God, Vikki, who challenges me daily and who loves me, protects me and comforts me. She is beautiful and was certainly a reward worth waiting for. Bro, you may be single, but hold on and trust God. I guarantee he will reward you.

Sort it out

- Take a look at the book of Mark, and check out how Jesus acted as a single bloke.
- Make a list of all the things you want to do in your life, your hopes, your visions and your dreams. Which of these would be affected if you were married?
- Regularly pray for your future wife, that God would protect her, deepen her relationship with him and continue blessing her.
- What aspects of your life need changing, growing and developing so that you can be the best for your future wife? Think about these and pray about them, then make a decision to change.

Big bruva

It is vital that we put the kingdom of God first. Are your desires for a girlfriend greater than your desires for a deep relationship with God? If they are, then your priorities need to change. Spend time with your big bruva and talk to him about the priorities that you have. Ask him to pray with you in surrendering your desires for a girlfriend to God, knowing that in his timing he will see your needs fulfilled. Work with your big bruva at putting God first and encourage him to keep checking up on you in this area.

Suddenly, during a conversation with one of my elders, things made sense. I was nearly thirty, older than all my friends. But I was the only one who was single. Everyone else was either married or engaged.

It wasn't that there hadn't been opportunities. I'd had a number of girlfriends. But nothing had worked out. I was no nearer to getting engaged than when I was twenty.

It was a time of transition in my life. I was about to give up a well-paid job, sell my house, change my lifestyle, follow God's calling and join Joshua Generation. With Joshua Generation, I would have to secure my own income through fundraising, hard work and God's provision.

When I talked it through with my elder, he simply said, 'Of course, this would be much harder had you been married or had children.' He was right. Being single had given me a tremendous freedom to serve God. I could commit in a way I may never have been able to had I been married.

One phrase that annoys me, although often said with love, is, 'One day God will bless you with marriage.' Really? I believe God is blessing me in my singleness. Don't get me wrong. If the right girl came along, I would love to get married. I often wish I were.

Being single is not always easy, but I know that God wants to use me in every circumstance of my life. I know that serving his purposes, not marriage, is the key to being content.

Michael Shaw, student associate, Joshua Generation
www.joshgen.org/associates/mikeshaw

10
for the love of men

It's summer. I am on the ministry team at a festival and it's hot as I pray for a teenage lad who is kneeling down, face in his hands, seemingly not allowing God to touch him. Worship continues and I start to pray, encouraging him that nothing can separate him from the love of God – that our sin cannot stand in God's way. As I speak these words, tears fall from his eyes and he starts to shake his head in disagreement. I continue to encourage him that God loves him, and as I do he breaks down uncontrollably, sobbing. It is obvious that this lad needs to be set free. I press into God and ask him to reveal to me the source of this deep pain and frustration. I start to share what I feel God is saying: 'God is showing me that you struggle with lustful thoughts about men; that you have homosexual thoughts.' The sobbing stops and his hands drop from his face as he looks at me completely baffled and responds, 'How did you know that? I have never told anyone . . .'

This revelation of a secret that only God and this lad could be aware of was confirmation to him of God's love for him. God wanted to be let into his life to touch him and heal him. Homosexuality is a sin. The Bible makes this very clear: 'Do not lie with a man as one lies with a woman; that is detestable' (Leviticus 18:22).

The Bible also makes it clear that homosexuality is rated equally alongside a whole bunch of other sins:

> Do you not know that the wicked will not inherit the kingdom of God? Do not be deceived: Neither the sexually immoral nor idolaters nor adulterers nor male prostitutes nor homosexual offenders nor thieves nor the greedy nor drunkards nor slanderers nor swindlers will inherit the kingdom of God. (1 Corinthians 6:9–10)

Despite their sin God still loves those who steal, those who swear, homosexuals, those who get angry, who lie, who are envious and those who dishonour their mother and father. God loves you! Some sections of society condemn and detest homosexuals and yet respect other wrongdoings including lying, sleeping around and drinking too much alcohol. God doesn't think like this; he puts us all in the same category – sinners. Dude, if you are thinking that you are not gay, and God sees others as worse than you, stop being naïve. If you are struggling with your sexuality and are thinking that God hates you because your sin is worse than everybody else's, stop being naïve. This is basic stuff. God so loved the world that he gave his only Son. We are all sinners, not one worse than the other. God has chosen to save us all, redeem us and bring us into a relationship with him through repentance of our sins and acceptance of the death and resurrection of Jesus. God, in his word, puts it a lot better than I do:

> But God demonstrates his own love for us in this: While we
> were still sinners, Christ died for us. (Romans 5:8)

You have heard this stuff before. God hates sin but loves the
sinner. As we look at the subject of sexuality, it is vital we all
start from this viewpoint. Bro, if you are struggling in this
area you will be feeling guilt, shame and condemnation; this
is not a good place to start from. Take a look at Chapter 1,
'Not guilty!' God has lavished his grace upon you and loves
you just as much as the next sinner, so let's deal with your
situation from this place of complete love and grace, and I
am confident that God can and will set you free.

Nature, nurture or irrelevant?

This classic debate has gone on for centuries. Are people
born homosexual or do they become homosexual through
the way their culture affects them? The truth is, scientists
haven't got a clue and no one actually knows. My question
is more important: Why would we want to know? OK, hear
me out. As a result of Adam and Eve disobeying God, sin
enters the world and human nature becomes corrupt. We do
stuff wrong that doesn't please God, whether this be lying,
stealing, lusting over images of men, swearing or any other
sin. When we come into a relationship with God and
discover that he is unhappy with the wrong we do, we seek
to please him and change. Jesus is our rad lad role model
and we should strive daily to live a lifestyle that resembles
his. Jesus didn't lie, steal, swear or lust over sexual images of
men, and neither should we. When we discover that God is
unhappy with something in our lives, we need to change it.

God is against the practice of homosexuality, and like

many other sins in our lives, this needs to be dealt with. If the Bible labels an aspect of our lifestyle as 'sin' then I believe that in God's power, grace and mercy he has the ability to heal us, change us and restore us. In him we can stop living out these sinful acts. As the typical argument goes, if homosexuality is a result of nature, we can convince ourselves that as we are born with it we cannot change – a valid reason we may think to continue to indulge in these sinful desires and actions. If homosexuality is a result of the way that we have been nurtured then we can change. If you have become something you can unbecome something, no matter how much counselling or help you may need. Bro, whatever the cause of homosexuality – nature or nurture – lustful thoughts and acts are sinful. It doesn't please God and damages his children, and by coming to Jesus he will help you change. One of the purposes of the life of Jesus was to help you to change and become whole. If you are struggling with homosexual lustful thoughts or actions, turn to Jesus. He is your counsellor and your strength and he can make you whole – whatever the source of these feelings.

The root: A broken image

If you practise homosexuality or have lustful thoughts over men you will probably be torn. You want to change while not wanting to at the same time. The apostle Paul knows full well where you are at:

> I do not understand what I do. For what I want to do I do not do, but what I hate I do. (Romans 7:15)

The truth is that you enjoy being sexually satisfied and

therefore you continue in this cycle of sin. In order to change it is essential to understand what motivates these desires. God does not view us according to our sexuality, whether we are heterosexual, homosexual or bisexual. He views us as people who are created in his image (Genesis 1:27). As a result of the Fall we have a deviant image. We are still made in the image of God, which is perfect, but we are tainted by the broken world that we live in and the sin that exists around us. Our deviant image seeks to live a bad lad lifestyle that doesn't please God. There is the perfect image of God and the imperfect image of our sinful nature, and there exists a gap in between. We need to seek continually to deal with this gap, to work through the brokenness of our image so that we can become more like Christ. We all have a deviant sexual nature to one degree or another, whether this is being a 'stud' who sleeps with as many girls in one week as possible, lusting after girls, or getting involved in porn. We all have a need which results in us trying to place our identity in our sexuality rather than in Jesus Christ. No worries; good news; Jesus saves the day: 'For the Son of Man came to seek and to save what was lost' (Luke 19:10).

Jesus came to find that lost part of you and restore it so that your character can be more like his and reflect God with a greater degree of truth. Ace! So what is your root? This is complex and we need to ask God to reveal to us where we have wrongly placed our identity so that we can change. There is one common gap that is a significant factor in problems of sexual identity – the 'cannibal compulsion'. I don't mean eating people, but those who need others who have the qualities they desire in themselves; the qualities they are missing. I have a gap in my sexual identity that I struggle with. When I was younger I found it difficult to see myself as a 'bloke'. I couldn't play football, or any sport for that matter, I didn't have a girlfriend and I didn't have a typical Hollywood-style body with muscles and a six-pack to go with it. Because of these factors I really struggled and continue to do so, because this is the part of me that is lost. Homosexuals, in this situation, instead of looking to Jesus to be their strength and support and to reaffirm their identity, look to other men. They engage in sexual conduct or lustful thoughts over those who form the 'character' that has the make-up of their gap.

Dude, if you are struggling with homosexual thoughts or practice you need to spend time with God and ask him to show you the root cause of your deviant image. As you discover this, the healing process will begin and you will start to find your identity in Christ rather than in your sexuality.

Do you enjoy your homosexuality?

If you are lusting over images of men and enjoy engaging in homosexual practice, it is evident to me that you have not fallen in love with Jesus. Once we fully appreciate that Jesus died on our behalf and paid the penalty for our sins, when we just get lost in a love for who he is, when the cross becomes real to us, we can't help but seek to change. You may think that homosexuality comes naturally to you. If this is the case it does not mean it is right: '. . . whoever loses his life for my sake will find it' (Matthew 10:39).

Do you enjoy what you are involved in? Drop it for a better life. Jesus says that if you lose that part of your life for his sake, then he will show you something more, something far better than the sin you have been involved in. That is awesome! Bro, no matter what sin we are involved with, if we find it exciting and we keep doing it, it is evident that we have not got lost in Jesus. When we come into the presence of God and we look into the eyes of Jesus, we meet with something that is far greater than the sin we entangle ourselves in – we find life. In the book of Revelation, the disciple John meets with God and his response is: 'When I saw him, I fell at his feet as though dead' (Revelation 1:17).

Dude, John met with God and he was blown away; he fell at his feet as if he was dead! Whatever sin we are tangled in, I believe that when we come face to face with God and with his Son Jesus, we meet with someone who will please us far better than the sin we are involved with.

Gazing into the eyes of Jesus

Sexual sin is not as difficult to deal with as we think it is, or would like it to be! The solution is simple: gaze into the eyes of Jesus. A woman slept around with heaps of blokes and the Pharisees caught her and brought her to Jesus, quoting an Old Testament law that said she should have rocks hurled at her in order to kill her. Our man Jesus replied, 'Whoever is without sin throw the first stone,' then he continued with what he was doing. John can tell the rest of the story better than I can:

At this, those who heard began to go away one at a time, the older ones first, until only Jesus was left, with the woman still standing there. Jesus straightened up and asked her, 'Woman, where are they? Has no one condemned you?' 'No one, sir,' she said. 'Then neither do I condemn you,' Jesus declared. 'Go now and leave your life of sin.' (John 8:9–11)

What was Jesus doing? This woman was addicted to sleeping around, but as she gazed into the eyes of Jesus his response was simply, 'Stop sinning.' Surely he had no understanding of how tough that is? But Jesus knew full well what he was saying. Once you gaze into the eyes of Jesus, something happens deep within and a healing takes place that is better than any therapy, counselling or psychiatrist. His response is simply, 'Sin no more.' Bro, it is actually that easy. You may have to spend some time dealing with your insecurities and gap, but in terms of the actual sin you commit, you can just stop.

Our real need

I have spoken to countless numbers of Christian lads who would call themselves 'gay' or who have said they struggle with homosexual thoughts. About 80 per cent of them are not gay at all. Society defines love for a girl as heterosexual and love for a bloke as homosexual. Nevertheless, you will see in Chapter 5 that there is a deep godly love that we can have and should have for our male friends around us. If we have love for a lad, society calls us gay. This is not God's way and therefore it is society that pigeonholes us into a homosexual box and lifestyle and we start to embrace these labels and live them out. Bro, it is OK to love lads and it is godly to have a deep love for them; this does not mean you are gay. If many 'gay' men accepted that it is OK to love a bloke, they would not take it that step further into lust or homosexual activity.

The subject of sexuality is not an easy one. There are more lads struggling in this area than let on, because it isn't 'cool'. If you are struggling with homosexual thoughts or desires, recognise that you are and start to deal with it. Surrender your sexuality to Jesus, let him be in control, and as you do this you will discover the reasons behind your motives. As God starts to heal you of your broken image, you will come to an understanding that your identity does not lie in your sexuality but in Jesus Christ. As you gaze into his eyes and behold his beauty, you will be compelled to become more like him. If you are struggling to be a rad lad in this area 'go and sin no more'.

Sort it out

- Our identity should be found in Christ and not in our sexuality. Take time just to be in the presence of Jesus and thank him for being a source of security you can completely trust.
- If you are struggling with homosexual thoughts or actions, list the reasons why this could be. What is comforting you? What is your gap? Write this list in the presence of God and ask him to guide you.
- Make a decision to be confident and tell someone about your struggles. It is not easy, but it is the rad lad thing to do.
- You may enjoy the thoughts or the practice. Before you move on, you have to recognise that this is wrong. Grab a concordance and see what the Bible really says.

Big bruva

Be brave enough to talk to your big bruva about the issues you have been facing – whether this involves actions or thoughts. The start of healing and growing in God is to confess your sin; a biblical thing

to do. Talk to your big bruva and share with him the list you have
made about why you think you may be having these thoughts – your
gap. Pray through these issues and ask your big bruva to help you
on the journey of gazing into the eyes of Jesus. Transformation will
occur.

My life had been evil moulded from an early age – it was like I was living in a world of my own that I couldn't understand. I remember when I was very young, below 10 years, and there was a lady who was staying with us. She was our housemaid. This lady used to play some funny sex games with me when we were alone, especially when she was bathing me. I never informed anyone and it really affected my life. Here in Kenya, especially then, children only came to learn about sex when they were adult, but I remember when I was in primary school I felt the urge for sex and used to masturbate often. When I went to high school I had a strong urge for sex, which was very abnormal. I used to feel it all the time and masturbation was the order of the day! I was also attracted to men and soon I met a fellow student with similar feelings and we had a sexual relationship for about three years. We would meet at midnight, drugged and possessed. Nobody was suspicious because I was well respected. When I finished high school I met a man and started another affair, but this time I was also involved in prostitution and had some girlfriends. Only at the hands of someone else did I feel loved. I changed from girlfriend to girlfriend and to prostitutes. My lifestyle affected my parents' reputation, but I didn't care. I ran away from home, and beer and women was the only life I knew and wanted. When I gave my life to Jesus and got married, things slowly began to change. It took a while and there was still further pain, but something was different. I had Christ in me and he was helping me out. I began to get a good team of faithful Christians around me who helped me, prayed with me and encouraged me, and I spent much time in the presence of God. It wasn't easy, but God healed me and delivered

140

me; he set me free. I want to encourage anyone in this same situation to stick with Christ. He can and will set you free.

Alex Maina, walk like Jesus walked Africa
www.wljw.org

11
only one chance

His life, work and determination so far have all been for this first rap battle. Nothing means more to him, and now he is on stage. It's the music, the moment; it's B Rabbit's one chance. The crowd go crazy as the battle begins. Little Titch is first up. The DJ spins and Little Titch piles insult after insult upon B Rabbit. 'They don't laugh 'cos he's white but 'cos he's white with a mic.' The crowd cheer these insults on and the 45 seconds are over. Now it's B Rabbit's turn. He takes the mic, is introduced and the DJ is told to start spinnin'. This is B Rabbit's moment and he gazes into the crowd. B Rabbit starts moving nervously to the beat and the crowd's cheers turn into name-calling. He gazes on as people are judging him and voices are screaming, 'White can't rap!' This is his one opportunity. He tries to own it but nerves have set in, people are dissin' him, his mind is telling him he ain't good enough and the crowd start shouting, 'Choke, choke!' as the music continues in the background. Fear has taken hold and he has missed his opportunity. The crowd go wild with laughter and B Rabbit is crushed.

Dude, have you seen *8 Mile*, loosely based on the life

story of Eminem? It is incredible. Eminem, as a non-Christian, has realised something we need to understand: we have one opportunity to do something with our life, to make it count. We all want to be somebody, to 'do' something. From an early age I remember praying that I wouldn't die without making a significant impact in many lives for God's glory. This is my desire and always has been. I have messed up on numerous occasions, but my desire remains the same. We are all on a search for personal significance, and as long as we are rooted in God there is nothing wrong with this, because it brings glory to God and that is the passion of his heart. God knows that as individuals we need a vision. We are told in Proverbs: 'If people can't see what God is doing, they stumble all over themselves' (Proverbs 29:18, *The Message*).

Without vision, we perish. Why? Vision changes things. Without vision, we wouldn't have the latest MP3 players, games consoles, cars or fashion items. Without vision slavery would not have been abolished, the education system would not exist and we would all be left to die from the latest flu epidemic. Without vision we don't progress as individuals either; we have nothing to wake up for in the morning; we have nothing that drives us. Without something we would like to achieve, we fill our time with things that damage us and we don't build anything for the future. Many lads without vision turn to drugs, alcohol, sex and violence in order to fill the endless void in their days. I respect any lad who has a vision and is working towards it. Whether you want to be a pop idol, a car mechanic, a footballer or the next Billy Elliot – it doesn't really bother me. If you are working towards a dream, you are seizing an opportunity that will make your life count.

Taking the dream?

The Bible documents a full-on history of God giving a heap of visions to rad lads. There is Joseph the dreamer, whose family tried to kill him, but ended up bowing down to him as they received the food he had stored up during the famine. Paul, after being converted to Christianity, had a one-track vision to preach the gospel across the continents in order to see many come to know the God who had changed his life. Let's get up to speed with what God is doing today!

In Acts, after the Day of Pentecost, the Holy Spirit turns up and crowds are gathered from across the continent, watching and listening in amazement as the disciples speak in other tongues and they hear an interpretation in their own language. Before this crowd Peter stands up, calls for silence, and then has a few words to say:

> In the last days, God says,
> I will pour out my Spirit on all people.
> Your sons and daughters will prophesy,
> *Your young men will see visions,*
> Your old men will dream dreams . . .
> (Acts 2:17–18, emphasis added)

Are you reading this book on a street paved with gold in heaven? No! Therefore we are still in the last days, and what does that mean? It means God is still giving his young men visions. God has a vision for your life. It is there for the taking; you can either make something of your life, giving glory to God, or you can merely exist. The choice is yours.

History defines you

You may be the type of lad who, on the face of it, doesn't care but deep down you have a desire to be something, although you haven't figured out what you want to do, who you want to be. You get into a right mess and get involved in other things to find your place of significance and worth, be it sleeping around, or getting involved in drugs, drink or a life of crime. Or perhaps you just don't bother, sign on the dole, go to bed late, get up late and live your life in a rut – merely existing rather than seeking God for the vision he has for your life.

You may fall under a different category – you just know you are going to 'make it' in some way, shape or form. You are pushy, confident and in pursuit of something. You know the vision God has for your life. We all have a friend who is one of these. I am one of them! If you are one of these lads you need to check your motives, where you are going and why you are going there. We will call these lads 'visionaries'. Whether you are the 'uninspired' sort or the 'visionary', you will be this way because of the way history has treated you and the way you have chosen to respond to it. You choose which category you are in; no one else does it for you.

You may be saying to yourself, 'Yeah, I hear you, but you don't know what I have been through!' It is that attitude that is stopping you from doing something with your life. We have all been through 'stuff', we all have a story to tell, and some stories are worse than others, but it is how you respond to your story that will define what you make of your life.

Let's get back to Eminem. This guy has had a tough life! His dad abandoned him when he was just a few months old, announcing he was gay; his mum branded him a thief while popping prescription pills. He was bullied at school so much that he was rushed to hospital, unconscious. In 'Cleaning out my closet' he says, 'My whole life I was made to believe I was sick when I wasn't.'

The dude has had a painful time. His life could have gone one of two ways. I am not saying that Eminem is perfect; he isn't, and neither am I! But what I am saying is that in his culture, with his painful experiences, he could have gone completely off the rails on alcohol, drug binges, sleeping around and violence – but did he? No. He decided to use his past to get his head down, work hard and make something of his life, something that would affect people in a positive way. Eminem is passionate that his existence is about something. He is open about his past in a way that changes the lives of his listeners. In 'Lose yourself' he says,

> Look, if you had one shot or one opportunity
> To seize everything you ever wanted – one moment
> Would you capture it or just let it slip?

Eminem has got hold of his life, has beaten it and overcome it in order to create a positive impact in the lives of the kids who listen to his music. Wicked! And this guy isn't even a Christian! Think what you could do with the same attitude with God at the centre. Dude, you may have been through some hard and painful stuff, just like Eminem, but you too have a choice as to how you respond to your history. Are you an uninspired lad? Do you have no aim or direction? Does your lack of aim and direction lead you to do things that you shouldn't be doing? God is fully aware that having no inspiration leads to an unfulfilled life, taking you down a path that heads nowhere and does much harm to yourself. The Bible talks about this:

> How long will you lie there, you sluggard?
> When will you get up from your sleep?
> A little sleep, a little slumber,
> a little folding of the hands to rest –
> and poverty will come on you like a bandit
> and scarcity like an armed man. (Proverbs 6:9–11)

I want to challenge those of you who are 'uninspired'. You may be happy about your life now, but if you look to the future – a struggle for money for your family; addictions to alcohol, laziness, drugs or lust – this is going to be damaging for you. Things have to change and they have to change today. Deep down you know they need to.

Freeze the moment

At the beginning of this book I talked about the whole *Mission Impossible* thing: 'Your mission, should you choose to accept it.' Bro, for you it may be now or never: either you start to change things about your life or you will self-destruct. You need to change the negative ways that your history has defined and moulded you into the person you are now. Your past has clung to you and you have not been free to walk into your future. You know the stuff I am talking about: the way you have been treated, let down by others, the negative words said over you, the laziness and the fears that you have. Our past acts as a barrier to the vision God has for us to walk in. Now it is time to freeze the moment, seize it and own it and get rid of the stuff that is holding you back. Quite simply, bro, you have to get over your past. It is hindering you, so let go. I think we make too much of a big deal of letting go. The problems we have can be our security blanket and our excuse for not moving on into what God has for us. I know that when I was in my bed, anorexic as a teenager, the attention that I was getting was great. I didn't want to change because I was feeling loved and this was building into my insecurities. For my own sake, no one else's, I had to change. Paul tells us how to change:

> Therefore, since we are surrounded by such a great cloud of witnesses, let us throw off everything that hinders and the sin that so easily entangles, and let us run with perseverance the race marked out for us. (Hebrews 12:1)

As a teenager, bullied and insecure, I thought there was some deep spiritual prayer I had to pray that would end all the pain and make my life better. There wasn't; it was simple. All I had to do was get before God and give him the things in my past that I found difficult, and then I had to let go of them. Once I had let go, I had to talk to a mate, and I was honest and talked everything through with him and he helped me. This did not mean that everything was instantly better, but it did mean that God was in control of the situation, not me – a great place to be in. Despite giving everything over to God, there were days when I still found it tough, and this was OK. God was still in control. When this happened, I just prayed and gave it back to him and then sought to work through it. Bro, God helped me let go of my past and walk into the vision he had for my life, and he wants to do the same for you.

Losing your life

We all have dreams as kids – to be a football player, a doctor, a fireman, to be famous. You may currently have a secret dream yourself that you are working towards. I have told you about my dream to be a children's TV presenter. It became an addiction. I would rush home every night, leaving behind the way that I was bullied and teased in order to get on my computer and print out a CV, to record another show reel to send off to casting directors across the UK, in the hope of convincing them I was going to be the next big thing.

I met with these casting directors, I gained as much work experience as possible behind the scenes of children's BBC, and I auditioned for commercials, soaps and television programmes. I got to a stage where there was hardly a casting director in the country who didn't know about me. I spent hundreds of pounds and heaps of time on getting my name out there, with a dream that one day the letter would come or the phone conversation would take place that would suddenly change everything, and fame, stardom and a television career would be mine. It was a buzz, a dream that I lived for. One sunny day, after a conversation with a children's BBC producer in London, I was on a natural high over where my career was heading; it was all going to be perfect. I was in my parents' garden sunbathing and thanking God, explaining that I loved him and would do anything for him. God bounced back with the ultimate question: 'Would you really do anything for me?' There was no need for endless contemplation! God sent his Son to die for my sins so that I could be in a relationship with him and would be eternally forgiven. Me doing anything for God was not much in return! Then God asked me to give up my dream to go into television. Shock. Horror. I didn't understand! There in my parents' garden, as I was chilling out on a sunny day, my whole future changed its course in an instant. God showed me that I was after a career in TV for the fame, the dosh. Any motivations centred on God were just not there at all. I had to surrender to his plans knowing that his path for my life was ultimately far better than mine.

Visions to do something with your life for God are great; you just need to make sure constantly that these visions are to glorify God. There are some big danger areas that lads can fall into, and I nearly fell into them all: girls, gold and glory. In a twenty-first-century world of *Pop Idol* winners who suddenly become millionaires, of football stars who have become international faces, of *Big Brother*, of *Fame Academy*, it is so difficult for lads to chase hard after Jesus, because we want to be somebody too. I know that place as I live in the same world as you. God has something to say: 'Whoever loses his life for me and for the gospel will save it' (Mark 8:35). If we lose our lives, all our dreams, the fame, the girls, the glory and the dosh, if we give it all up in pursuit of what God wants, then the Bible says that we will find life itself. All that stuff isn't actually life; it is what we think life is. True life is giving everything up for God and living a life that is for him alone. As we do this we will find out what 'life' actually means. This has certainly been my experience.

After letting go of my own dreams, I went to uni and studied theology, I started a ministry with the aim of challenging people to 'walk like Jesus walked', I got married to a beautiful woman of God, we launched a youth magazine and started to speak at events across the country. Not one step of the way has been easy; there have been financial pressures; there have been times when I have wanted to quit because it's too hard; there have been times when I have not felt able to do the task in hand, and there have been times when I have secretly thought that I should have pursued my television career after all, because the money would have been very handy! However, I completely love what I do because I know that it pleases God. I am doing what he wants me to do. As I continue on this journey I am starting to find this real life that Jesus speaks about.

As you seek God on the dream he has for your life, grab as much time with him as possible – make sure your motives are focused on him. Sometimes you will slip, but that's OK – this is part of it. Just make sure you keep refocusing yourself and the vision so that you are working towards his glory only.

Even young men stumble

As you let go of your past and look towards God for the vision he has for your life, remember that there will be occasions when you will get it wrong. Use these times to grow and learn, and admit to yourself and others that you have got it wrong. Humility is the key. Bro, there have been times when I have got it wrong: I have treated people bad, let people down, I have said the wrong stuff and had the wrong motives. These were hard times. When these things happen, get into God. Isaiah 40 tells us:

> Even youths grow tired and weary,
> and young men stumble and fall;
> but those who hope in the LORD
> will renew their strength.

> They will soar on wings like eagles;
> they will run and not grow weary,
> they will walk and not be faint. (Isaiah 40:30–31)

I am learning a very important truth. In the past, when I have got it wrong, I have tried to fix these mistakes in my own strength. Don't! When you get things wrong, go and spend time with God, pray, put hope in him, and he will renew your strength and show you a way forward. Dude, in my own life I would rather run for the vision that God has given me and get things wrong than never mess up because I am not running for anything of any importance at all. I want to encourage you to do the same. We learn from our mistakes, and I am learning fast!

Whether you are the sort of lad who is a visionary or the sort of lad who is generally uninspired, I want to inspire you to change, to run for the vision that God has for your life and to ensure that your sole motivation is to see God glorified. A rad lad isn't simply someone who preaches in front of the masses, who is on some main stage as a worship leader or an actor on our TV screens. A real rad lad is someone who seizes every opportunity, every moment in his life, and lives it for Jesus Christ. Bro, start making your life count.

Sort it out

- Write down the gifts God has given you, the things he has made you good at.
- Write down the vision you feel God may have for your life. It doesn't matter whether this seems silly or funny, or whether you ever get there. Just write down what you feel God is saying for now.

- Are you an uninspired lad or a visionary? Write down what aspect of your past has moulded you into this sort of person.
- Think about what aspects of your life and character need to change so that you can run for the vision God has given you.

Big bruva

Show these lists to your big bruva and ask him to pray with you over the things that hinder you and that you need to throw off. Pray about this together and say a final, once-and-for-all goodbye to them. Then ask your big bruva to question you continually on these areas in order to help you grow and change. Finally, be honest with your big bruva and share with him your hopes and dreams, the vision you feel God has for your life, and then ask him to help you start to reach these goals. Write down some mini-goals first – little steps towards helping you to achieve this vision.

Respect to rad lad

Many people have had a dream, a dream that will change the world. Christians dream of something big, of impacting cities, nations and continents. This is a good dream but a dream that is for the few as opposed to the many. I change the world – a bold but true statement! I go to uni and live in halls of residence, living with about 80 other lads. It took time but I have developed a friendship with each of them and they know about my faith. I am now at the place where lads knock on my door for advice, for prayer or just for support. Some lads knock because they have run out of money and don't know what to do; we pray together and God provides. Other lads have serious issues that they are facing; we pray and I help out where I can or point them in the right direction. One lad had split up with his girlfriend and had turned to alcohol. He was on the edge and stated that he wanted to commit suicide. He was depressed, lonely and hurt. I became his mate, we hung out together, went to the cinema together, talked and got to know each other. I showed him the same love that Jesus Christ had shown me. I recently got a letter off this friend that said:

> I have read in the Bible where Jesus challenged his 'followers' who claimed to live for him. Jesus says to them, 'When I was hungry you did not feed me; when I was sick you did not care for me; when I was thirsty you did not give me a drink.' I don't know God but I know that he knows you and Jesus will not be telling you that you 'did not' do something for him. All I can say is thank you – you have changed my world.

You see, we all have the potential to change worlds. How many worlds are you changing?

Darren Short, student

154

12

watchin' ya words

I'm walking through town and see Jay walking towards me. 'Oi di**head!' I shout, just for a laugh. He comes over and asks me what I am up to. The truth is that I just wanted to go for a walk, possibly get a newspaper and a can of my fave carbonated beverage. Not very exciting and certainly not impressive! My tongue starts to speak on my behalf as I explain that there I was, working away, when God prompted me to go outside. As I left my house God directed me to two homeless guys. I chilled with them and they asked me what I did, which naturally led to a full-on gospel Power-Point presentation along the theme that they were lost and needed to be saved. I continue to explain how these home-less guys then said that they would think about the need for Jesus as their personal Lord and Saviour – the story evolving in my head of these guys falling face down on the floor with wailing and repenting seems just a bit too far fetched! Jay's eyes are wide open, his jaw drops and he stands in awe at the picture I have just painted. He walks away thinking how great I am and how close to God I must be. OK, I quickly justify the situation to myself . . . I was praying while I was working at my desk, I did come out of the house and I did chat to the homeless guys. No lies, just slight exaggerations. In Jay's eyes I am almost an apostle of biblical proportions and no one is harmed. Sorted!

Let me just state that the scenario above did not happen; it is just fiction. But it could easily have taken place if I wasn't working so hard to seek to honour God in the way that I use my tongue. In one swift swoop, I would have put my mate down through swearing and then made up a whole concoction of lies to gain respect in his eyes! Bro, we need to watch our words, whether those words come out of our mouths or our fingers as we send text messages and write e-mails. Whether you are in town, at the pub, at school, at work or on the football pitch, it is vital that you honour God with the words that you use. Do you?

Lad banter

Ever been in town with your mates when you see a nice-looking girl and point her out to your mates as a 'fit bird' or declare that you could 'have a bit of that'? Ever gone up to your mates and started a conversation that goes along the lines of, 'Man, you'll never guess what (enter name of person you are just about to criticise, judge, condemn or gossip about) did today . . .'? Have you ever got annoyed with a game on your console and shouted a heap of swear-words at this inanimate object, or heard some shocking news only to respond, 'Jesus Christ!'? Perhaps you compulsively stretch the recital of stories far beyond the realms of reality as you sit over a pint with your mates in the pub? Or do you engage in the classic lad scenario where you 'put down' your mates in order to gain a laugh, some respect, or to make yourself feel better in the presence of others? In all honesty I struggle with each of these and Vikki has to make sure she holds me accountable in the way I use my tongue. There is one area I find particularly difficult, though . . . the dissin'! It's just so easy! So, there I am with my mates, chilling, relaxing and having fun, and a mate cracks a joke aimed at me. Without much thinking I jump into action with a quick-fire response, my mate knows his place and I get a laugh. Nice one, Mark! Actually, not nice at all – far from it. Bro, have you ever had a friend you trusted lie to you or put you down in front of others? Remember how painful it was? Remember how hurt, low and completely gutted you were at the way those you thought were mates treated you? Bro, you use your tongue in ways that are wrong and so do I. We need to stop. Let's check out what the Bible says and this time, once and for all, let's deal with it. Are you joining me?

Disrespectin' God

Remember calling a parent by their first name? I do! Third world war kicked off along with a command never to call my dad by his name again! Blasphemy is pretty much the same but worse, and kicking off war with God isn't a clever idea. Have you ever shouted 'Oh my God' when your mates told you something, or got annoyed that the ball hit the goal post and shouted the name of your Lord and Saviour in a completely irreverent way? God is not happy about the way we use his name and he is well protective of it. God won't be dissed. He doesn't want us disrespecting him: he made sure it was in his top ten list of don'ts. In at number four:

No using the name of GOD, your God, in curses or silly banter;

GOD won't put up with the irreverent use of his name. (Exodus 20:7, *The Message*)

Using God's name in this way does not honour him. He has politely asked for us not to do it, so don't. I called my dad Paul and in that split second afterwards, as I watched his blood boil and his face turn red, I knew I should not have done it. This situation with my dad was pretty bad – if God won't put up with the way I use his name, I really don't want to find out what that means! I need to stop. Bro, so do you!

Blinking heck, flip and you'll never guess what!

Whether it is in anger on the pitch, when we get with the lads, or aimed at someone we are particularly annoyed with, we fire out the occasional or frequent swearword. This isn't good. Although the swearwords themselves are a problem, we also need to look at the motive behind them. There are too many Christians out there, and I do this too, who exchange a swearword for a more 'holy' word like 'blinking heck' or 'flip', or who even swear in a foreign language just to ease the guilt. Whether it is a swearword or another word in exchange, we are speaking out of a place in our heart that is not right with God. Therefore our words do not bring honour to God and the world will hold us accountable. Have you ever sworn and had someone around you chuck out that annoying comment, 'And you, a Christian! I thought you didn't swear!' You hold your breath and count to ten in order to refrain from offering this person a few more choice words, but the truth is, you know they are right.

Aren't girls gossips? Bro, so are you! Gossiping isn't a 'girl' thing, it is a human thing. Dictionary.com defines gossiping in the following way: 'Rumour or talk of a personal, sensational, or intimate nature.' I am convinced that youth groups are the best greenhouses in which to grow gossips. Whether it is rumours about our church leader, someone in the youth group or a new person to the church, we like to spread a story. Bro, this needs to stop. Have you ever been on the receiving end of a rumour that is being spread like wildfire? It is hurtful. It is far too common in the Christian world for a situation to be told in confidence, only for this trust to be broken and the story spread like Chinese whispers along the way. If you gossip you need to make a decision to stop today, and to honour God with the way you speak about those around you.

The book of Colossians gives us some sound advice on how we should use our language: 'Let your conversation be always full of grace, seasoned with salt . . .' (Colossians 4:6). Paul says that our words should draw people – there should be a flavour about the things we say that attracts people and ultimately points them to God. Swearing does not attract people and certainly does not point them to God. It is far too easy to swear. I struggle with this myself, but I desperately want God to be pleased with the words that I use and I want my speech to point people to my God – don't you? I can try to convince myself that God doesn't really mind. What's the big deal? But I get into his presence, I spend some time with him and I know in my heart that God is not happy with these words that I say. Bro, God isn't happy with our swearing. Let's seek to change our language for him, because we love him.

Lies, all lies

Hands up, who has lied? Every person reading this book will have lied; we all do. A snake lied to Adam and Eve and they were consequently chucked out of the Garden of Eden. Their sin led to the sin of mankind. The Bible tells us that Satan is a liar:

> You belong to your father, the devil, and you want to carry out your father's desire. He was a murderer from the beginning, not holding to the truth, for there is no truth in him. When he lies, he speaks his native language, for he is a liar and the father of lies. (John 8:44)

Satan encourages us to lie for our own benefit. We may get something out of the lying, whether this be financial or a gift; a lie might save us from getting into trouble or make us look better in someone else's eyes. If we are not careful, days can be filled with a series of mini-lies, from covering up why we haven't done our homework to lying to our parents about the fact that we have been drinking, smoking or anything else. Lying goes against the very nature of God because God is truth, therefore when we lie, as children of God, we damage the reputation of God and this just isn't on!

Have you ever met anyone who is just one of those compulsive liars? I remember there was a girl at my school who was pregnant one week, not the next, and then her mum was pregnant a week later, and the week after that she was allegedly dying of cancer! Although this was funny at the time, it is such a sad place to be in – a web of lies which can lead to such destruction. However, these big lies started with small ones and I don't want to see any lad reading this book ever get to that place of being a compulsive liar. Deep down you know when you are heading along that track. I want to encourage you to deal with any problem you may have with lying – tackle it head on, today. Agreed?

Compulsive lying starts with smaller lies, and I want us to deal with three areas of lying: social lying (flattery), white lies and intentional deceit. Have you ever told a girl that she looked great but went away telling your mates a completely different story? Or have you ever told a mate he is a great footballer, when you know that you actually think he is rubbish? No matter how much we think we are helping people with our forms of flattery, it is still lying and ultimately it is not beneficial for the other person. Bro, if you are involved in this form of social lying, Psalm 62 speaks directly about you: '. . . they take delight in lies. With their mouths they bless, but in their hearts they curse' (Psalm 62:4). This isn't honouring to God, it is still lying and ultimately it is not building up other people. Sort it out. Find something positive to say that's honest; or, if you really can't, change the subject!

Little white lies

You know the ones – 'My dog ate my homework', 'I feel ill and need a day off work', or even unintentional lies such as, 'Yes Dad, I will pay you back!' Some of these white lies we say in order to cover ourselves or protect other people. Some white lies are based on a promise you make and never keep; perhaps you had no intentions of keeping that promise in the first place. I am for ever telling Vikki I will wash the dishes before I go to bed, or I will only have one pint when I am out, but do I stick to this? No. Do I mean what I say? Yes, but not enough to actually follow through with it! We have to be careful with white lies. We convince ourselves that they are OK, but they aren't. I would also place exaggerating under 'white lies'. If we go back to my introduction, I told a series of exaggerations which were dramatic extensions of what had actually happened. This is lying too!

Have you ever been in a situation where someone has assumed something pretty impressive about you, and you have let them carry on thinking that instead of telling them the truth? This is intentional deceit. I wanted to be a TV presenter, remember? I got involved in working behind the scenes of a live children's TV programme. I was only a runner, which meant that I did all the jobs no one else wanted to do. It was the bottom of the bottom, but when people saw me walk around with my BBC bag I certainly allowed them to assume that I was something more than I actually was! This was intentional deceit with an impressive BBC bag to go with it; this is lying too. We are told that '. . . no lie comes from the truth' (1 John 2:21).

We can convince ourselves all we like, but any form of lying is wrong because it is not 'of the truth'. Instead of saving ourselves, we should confess our sin and deal with it. Instead of trying to impress our mates through flattery, we should be honest about their true qualities and help them to grow in those qualities. Instead of promising to do something and not doing it, we should keep to our promises. Instead of allowing people to assume things about us, we should explain the truth, even if it means we look a little less impressive in their eyes. Lying does not reflect the truth that is at the very heart of the character of God, and when we lie we misrepresent the character of God to a world that needs to know him. Bro, lying is wrong. Deal with it and stop.

Dissin' ya mates

This is far too easy! We banter with our mates, which usually takes the form of dissin' each other. We pick on our mates' appearance, abilities, inabilities, sense of style, character flaws and anything else about them that we can turn into a comeback that will put them down and make everyone else around them laugh. I struggle with this because I am quite good at it! Bro, do you do this? God has been speaking to me very clearly on this subject and it needs to be sorted. When we become a Christian we enter into a love relationship with God. We fall in love with him, and in turn the love of God should be burning in us for those who are around us. Dissin' people does not show the love of God, even if it is funny.

We also diss our mates through getting annoyed and hurling out angry responses and words. Have you ever sent a text message that is full of abuse or written an e-mail in anger? I have received numerous e-mails that have caused me to get angry. I used to fire back, out of anger. I am now at a stage where I pray, lay down my anger and seek God for his wisdom on how to respond – this means no swearwords and no bitterness, but love and grace instead. The Bible speaks heaps about love and how our response should be when we love people. Corinthians tells us that love is not rude (1 Corinthians 13:5). Is the way we speak to our friends when we diss them rude? Of course it is. Corinthians also tells us that love builds up (1 Corinthians 8:1). Does our dissin' build up in this way? Of course it doesn't.

A matter of the heart

Liar, Liar is one of my all-time favourite films. Fletcher (Jim Carrey) is a lawyer and a bad father whose son makes a wish that he cannot lie. The wish comes true and suddenly Fletcher finds he can only speak the truth. In one particular scene Fletcher arrives at work and can only reply with his honest thoughts to everyone he meets! One female member of staff with a shocking haircut says, 'Do you like my new dress?' The response: 'Anything to keep the focus off your head.' His next victim turns around and asks, 'How are you, Fletcher?' He replies, 'You're not important enough to remember.' Finally a rather large dude shouts, 'What's up, Fletcher?' and he is met with a truthful reply: 'Your cholesterol, fatty!' OK, so it's a funny film, but imagine if you could not lie – would that change the comments you make during your day? It certainly would change mine, and this should not be the case. Whether it is blaspheming, lying, dissin' or swearing, whatever is stored up in our hearts is what comes out of our mouths. 'For out of the overflow of the heart the mouth speaks' (Matthew 12:34).

We can put on our Christian front, but it is in the face of adversity – when someone annoys us and we swear, when we need to cover our backs so we lie, when we seize the opportunity to diss a mate and get a laugh, or when we hurt ourselves and blaspheme – that what is really stored up in our hearts comes out of our mouths. Bro, you may not think this is a pretty big issue, but it is. The Bible says that the way we use our words sets the direction for our whole body and our whole lifestyle:

Take ships as an example. Although they are so large and are driven by strong winds, they are steered by a very small rudder wherever the pilot wants to go. Likewise the tongue is a small part of the body, but it makes great boasts. Consider what a great forest is set on fire by a small spark. The tongue also is a fire, a world of evil among the parts of the body. It corrupts the whole person, sets the whole course of his life on fire, and is itself set on fire by hell. All kinds of animals, birds, reptiles and creatures of the sea are being tamed and have been tamed by

man, but no man can tame the tongue. It is a restless evil, full
of deadly poison. (James 3:4–7)

It is clear that our mouths should be used to honour God
and build up our mates, so how do we stop lying? First, if the
mouth speaks out of the overflow of the heart then we need
to assess what is in our hearts. We lie out of a proud and fearful heart, a desire to be loved and respected, and sometimes
a need to save ourselves from a sin that we have committed.
Our heart is in a wrong place with God and the consequence
is ungodly talk. We need to get into God. If you spend time
placing your heart in God through prayer, worship and reading the Bible, then it will be the things of God that will
consume your heart and positive words, encouraging
comments and words of praise will flow from your mouth.

Second, the Bible makes some sound comments on this
matter: 'It's not what you swallow that pollutes your life,
but what you vomit up' (Matthew 15:11, *The Message*). You
see, it is a decision of the heart. We live in a non-Christian
culture that is full of bad language, gossip, slander, swearing
and blasphemy. We hear it all around us on a daily basis, and
it enters our ears, eyes and consequently our hearts. We can't
help that, and even if we ran away from the world and
locked ourselves in a room 24/7, it would not deal with the
source of the problem. We can't help what goes in, but as
this verse says, we can help what comes out. It is easy to send
a text in anger, to swear at a mate, or in the heat of a situation to lie to get out of a problem. Nevertheless, when the
heat is on we should give ourselves a few seconds and decide
in our hearts to respond in the right way – in grace, love and
truth – and then follow through with this decision.

Bro, we need to seek to be rad lads in the way that we use

our tongues. We need to speak with consistency, integrity and in love in order to build up those around us and point them towards growth and maturity in Jesus. This is the theory. The rest is up to you.

Sort it out

- Spend time with God and confess the wrong ways in which you use your words. Ask for his forgiveness.
- Make a decision to use your words in a godly way. Tell your friends around you and ask them to pick you up on this when you get it wrong. Listen to them and be accountable; they will help you grow.
- Spend some time reading 1 Corinthians, which explains how true love acts. Seek to implement this in your life.
- Spend some time with God. As your heart engages with his you will naturally start to speak out of an overflow of a changed heart.

Big bruva

It is important that we have people around us who hold us accountable for our words and actions, ensuring that they are godly. Be honest and talk to your big bruva about how you struggle with your words, whether this be lying, dissin', gossiping, etc. Ask your big bruva to pray with you, help you and encourage you to get this area of your life right before God.

Respect to rad lad

Let's face it, we want respect and we will stop at nothing to get it. That includes using our words in the wrong way. When I was younger I was a compulsive liar. I would like to save myself when I knew I was going to get into trouble; I would also lie for the sake of it, for attention and respect. However, on one occasion enough was enough and I knew it had to stop.

It was lunchtime at school and we were all in the playground. I was a well respected lad, good at sport and good with the ladies, if you know what I mean! On this occasion I got carried away and told my mates that one of the teachers fancied me and that she touched my bum in the classroom. My mates were blown away. She was liked by heaps of lads and they were laughing and joking, but for my best mate these lies were enough. My mate went up to the teacher in question and asked her outright. Of course she said it was not true, and she was right. I was then marched into the headmaster's room along with this teacher in order to explain the whole scenario. I was asked whether I wanted to take this sexual harassment story further and I knew that I had to tell the truth; this had gone too far. I was suspended on the spot for a week and I walked out of that room thinking that my best mate was truly my best mate. Of course I was annoyed, but if it hadn't stopped here, who knows what would have happened?

Do you get tempted to lie? Find a mate and tell him. Ask him to pray with you and encourage you and if he hears you telling a lie ask him, in private, to challenge you on it. We need people around us who will challenge us to become more godly. I certainly did! It isn't honouring to use our tongues in the wrong way. It doesn't reflect the image of God. If you are having problems, get it sorted now.

Jason Holmes, student

13
stressed out man

What a day at college – glad to have finished! Teachers going on about how my work isn't good enough and how I will never make the grade; my mates unhappy with me because I can't play at the band's gig this Friday. I should just try and forget it all as I walk home, but no: I get through the door and remember that my A-level coursework has to be in tomorrow. Flip, how did I forget that? I am also supposed to be working tonight. Argh! I can't be in two different places doing two different things at once! What am I going to do? And now my girl is also on my mobile asking whether we can spend time together. Stress! To top it all off, my mum walks in and starts screaming about how I promised to tidy my room a few days (or was it weeks?) ago. I feel like I have had enough. Too much to do, don't know where to start. Why is life full of so much stress? Sometimes I just want to run!

Have you ever felt that way? The dictionary definition of stress is 'to be subject to physical or mental pressure, tension, or strain' (dictionary.com). This is harsh stuff and for us lads this can come in many forms: stress from society about the way we should look; stress from parents, college, work; girlfriend trouble or hormones going crazy and bringing stresses of their own; and let's not forget the stress that we place on ourselves through wrong actions and bad choices! We live in a world of stress and I would love to tell you that it gets easier, but it doesn't. Have you ever seen Stressed Eric? Eric is a cartoon character whose days are filled with stress. Every time he is met with stress a vein in his cartoon head pulsates. The website stressederic.com explains the story behind this guy's life:

> Eric is 40, and lives in London. He is a middle class single father (divorced) with two kids and a crippling mortgage. His son is so dim he's been kept back at school three years running. His daughter is frail and allergy ridden. His wife has left him for a Buddhist and his au pair is an unreliable waster. Even the family next door are successful and wealthy, a stressful reminder of what his life could have been.

Do you have a metaphorical vein in your head that pulsates under pressure, or do you lash out, get angry and get involved in ungodly action? Bro, deal with it now. If life is stressful for you, it is not going to change. You don't hit a certain age and it all gets better, guaranteed – ask your parents or check out Stressed Eric! However, we can change our attitude towards stress and how we deal with it, and we can actually start to use stress in order to see our lives grow in character and develop in maturity in God. Bro, stress is here to stay. Don't run away. Let's deal with this together and learn to become godly in the way we handle the stress that hits our lives. I guarantee that your life will be much better for it.

'I'm so stressed'

Has that ever been your response to the 'how are you doing?' question? I remember spending a large chunk of my teenage years feeling pretty much stressed out, and whenever anyone asked me how I was doing I was 'stressed'. For me there were two particular areas that brought along high levels of stress – being bullied and the view I had of myself. These two areas were very much linked. I remember one day at school, walking through the playground to taunts, jibes and lads making comments about my skinny body. At the end of the day I went home, and ran into the house to look in the mirror – and the words of these bullies had begun to take effect as I saw something weak, skinny and ugly. This piled on the stress and the result was a long-term outbreak of spots that only fuelled the bullying and heightened the stress. Hormones plus stress can result in a classic outbreak of teenage acne! However, there are other indicators that inform us that we are suffering from stress, and knowing these tell-tale signs will enable us to deal with stress more effectively earlier on, reducing its effects over our life long term. Here are some classic signs of stress:

- irritability
- difficulty sleeping
- going off your food
- becoming quiet and withdrawn
- feeling tired all the time
- stomach aches or headaches
- finding it hard to concentrate on your work
- having difficulty solving problems you usually find easy

The next time someone asks you how you are doing and your response is 'stressed', take a look at this list and see whether these symptoms are present in your life. If they are, use this knowledge to work towards dealing with stress in a rad lad way.

The source of stress

Once we are aware of the root of our stress we are in a better position to deal with it. We need to understand that God is not a God of confusion, but a God of peace (1 Corinthians 14:13). The world that God created was the peaceful, tranquil Garden of Eden in which he placed Adam and Eve. Adam and Eve sinned big time when they ate from the tree of the knowledge of good and evil. Once they had disobeyed God in this way, peace was exchanged for hard work and a stressful environment:

> Cursed is the ground because of you;
> through painful toil you will eat of it
> all the days of your life. (Genesis 3:17)

Painful toil sounds like stressful work to me, and stress has been around from that day on! There are two primary sources of twenty-first-century stress: internal and external. Let's start with internal. Bro, you need to realise that some of your stress comes from the bad decisions you make. This could be because you are disobeying the word of God, God's voice, or because you are making plain stupid and unwise choices!

Stressed out by your own actions (internal)

A friend of mine fancied this girl who seemed real nice but wasn't the long-term partner God had for him. The relationship started off well, but it soon slipped into chaos as arguments erupted. He loved this girl and didn't want to let go, but in the secret place, during his time with God, he knew that God had told him to let her go. But he didn't. His emotions enabled him to think that he knew what was best for his life over the thoughts of Creator God! Then my friend found out that this girl had been seeing another lad behind his back, and he was broken. During the course of the relationship and afterwards, my friend was pretty stressed out. Of course he was: he had disobeyed God.

I remember the first year of my GCSEs. It took me all that first year to realise that these exams were pretty important and it was only then that I decided to work. Know that place? I had to pile two years of GCSE work into one year and the stress this created was immense – all caused by my own foolish decisions, computer playing and time wasting instead of putting effort into my work.

Do you remember the Old Testament story of David? This guy disobeyed the law of God. He slept with another man's wife and then killed her husband. It doesn't take a grade A student to work out the result. Stress! Psalm 51 is great; check it out. It gives a full account of the stress that David was going through and how he turned back to God. Here is a snippet:

> Let me hear joy and gladness;
> let the bones you have crushed rejoice. (Psalm 51:8)

The guy was completely gutted. The turmoil and stress he was facing were immense. When we become Christians we invite the Spirit of God into our lives, and when we live a lifestyle that displeases God and is contrary to his word, his Spirit starts to tell us this and our human response is to feel stressed – just like David did, who felt that his bones had been crushed. We often go around declaring that we are stressed. We get worked up and are faced with the challenge of dealing with how we feel, when a few wise choices, listening to God and obeying his word, would eliminate this stress.

Stressed out by the actions of others (external)

Even if we do pretty well at eliminating the majority of the stress we cause ourselves, there is always someone else who will give us a hand to ensure that our life isn't completely stress free! This could be parents, friends, lecturers, or the huge queue at your local video shop. A major source of stress for lads can be exams, which has resulted in a high number of student suicides. The Samaritans have stated,

> The largest group of males who attempt suicide are aged between 20 and 24. Suicide, second to accidents, is the largest cause of death in 15–24 year old men. 56% of young men who attempt suicide have employment or study problems. (The Samaritans, 2003)

However, Christian lads face certain stresses of their own. There is a stress that comes with being a Christian – the pressure to get it right and live the right 'godly' lifestyle. This pressure comes from parents, youth leaders, church leaders and grannies in the church who have prayed for us for years. This pressure can be immense, and we need to learn how to deal with it in a godly way.

Blowing a fuse

Bro, how do you respond to stress? I tend to get sulky and withdrawn and don't talk to anyone. I bottle it all up until there comes a point when I've had enough and just let it all blow. This results in anger, shouting and a few choice swear-words. Ask Vikki! Not really a rad lad response. We all deal with stress differently, but I can guarantee that however we handle it, if we are not focused on God, our response will be ungodly. How do you respond? Do you get on line and start surfing for porn? Do you go to the pub and drink as much alcohol as you can, to dull the pain and forget about your stress? Perhaps you lash out, get angry and start beating up things or people. I remember seeing a friend of mine at uni whose response to stress was to bang his head violently on the wall. He didn't want to hurt other people, so he hurt himself. Some of us handle stress through self-harm, cutting our bodies or developing eating disorders and keeping it secret from the rest of the world. Lads, if you are blowing a fuse and responding to stress in any of these ways, this will only get worse as you grow older. Let's get it sorted before God – now.

Dealing with stress: purpose, prayer, perspective, promise

Whether it is down to internal or external sources, we all get stressed. Sadly, because of the fall of man, it is a fact of life. I want us lads to grow together as we seek to deal with stress in a rad lad way. Make a decision now to stop responding to stress in the way that you do. God has been speaking to me through the book of James and has been teaching me some key principles for dealing with stress in a rad lad way. Let's take a look.

The purpose of stress

> Consider it pure joy, my brothers, whenever you face trials of many kinds, because you know that the testing of your faith develops perseverance. Perseverance must finish its work so that you may be mature and complete, not lacking anything. (James 1:2–4)

What? A purpose to stress? Yes! As Christians we are called to be more like Christ, to walk like Jesus walked. A great quote from *The Discipline of Grace* conveys this well:

> The Holy Spirit's work of transforming us more and more into the likeness of Christ is called sanctification. Our involvement and co-operation with Him in His work is what I call the pursuit of holiness. That expression is not original with me. Rather, it is taken from Hebrews 12:14, 'Make every effort [literally: pursue] . . . to be holy; without holiness no one will see the Lord.' (Jerry Bridges, *The Discipline of Grace*, Navpress 1994)

God desires that we become more like his Son Jesus. The result of our striving for holiness is that those around us will see a difference – they will see God. Bro, I know this sounds crazy, but as James says, consider it pure joy when you are going through stress because, dealt with in the right way, this will enable you to become more like Jesus. When a source of stress hits you in the face, don't use expletives, blow a fuse and go crazy. Have a right attitude, tackle it head on and use it to help you grow in character and in your relationship with God.

Praying when stressed

If any of you lacks wisdom, he should ask God, who gives generously to all without finding fault, and it will be given to him. But when he asks, he must believe and not doubt, because he who doubts is like a wave of the sea, blown and tossed by the wind. That man should not think he will receive anything from the Lord; he is a double-minded man, unstable in all he does. (James 1:5–8)

Bro, here is the crunch, the key, and this is where you and I need to change. What happens when stress hits us? We get stressed out and we choose an ungodly way of handling it. James gives solid advice: if you are feeling stressed, your first response should be to get into God, get into his presence, spend time with him and pray. In a stressful situation, when you are about to lose it and go crazy, you should jump into God and your first prayer should be to hand the problem, the stressful situation, over to Jesus. This is exactly what 1 Peter 5:7 tells us to do: 'Cast all your anxiety on him because he cares for you.' This is amazing stuff. God is so interested in you, and he cares for you so much, that he doesn't want you to feel the way you do when stress hits you. He wants you to give it over to him instead: he is big enough, he can handle it!

So, first prayer, give over your stress to God. Second prayer, ask for wisdom. Once we have handed the stress, concern and worry to God, there will be times when we then need wisdom with regard to what to do next. Take my friend in the earlier example. God told him that his girl was not for him. If he had prayed for wisdom, God would have told him the best way to handle the situation and he would have finished the relationship. Or your mum and dad could be arguing, and this could be very stressful for you. Once you have prayed and given your stress over to God, you should then pray for wisdom. God may tell you to talk to your parents, or he may tell you to go and talk to somebody else about the situation.

Whatever stress hits your life, no matter how big or small, God knows that it is coming and if you pray and ask for wisdom James 1:5 tells you that God will give it. This wisdom will be the best way for you to solve the problem. This verse in James also says that once we ask for wisdom we should believe and not doubt. We need to trust that what God has said to us *is* his wisdom.

Let's get back to my mate. He spent time with God and he knew that this girl was not right, but he didn't trust the wisdom God had given him. The result was pain and stress when he realised she had been in a relationship with another bloke behind his back. When we come to God and ask for wisdom, James says that he will give it. Despite our emotions and what we think we want, we need to trust God's wisdom and act upon his advice. This will bring down the amount of stress that we hit in our lives. Good call!

Keeping a perspective on stress

The brother in humble circumstances ought to take pride in his high position. But the one who is rich should take pride in his low position, because he will pass away like a wild flower. For the sun rises with scorching heat and withers the plant; its blossom falls and its beauty is destroyed. In the same way, the rich man will fade away even while he goes about his business. (James 1:9–11)

When we are involved in our stressful situations they can seem so big to us, but if we gain a wider perspective they are usually not so big at all. When we realise that our circumstances are not as stressful as we think, they are far easier to deal with. Dr Walter Cavert conducted a scientific survey of stress and came up with the following statistical conclusion about things that stress us out:

Things which never happen: 40 per cent
Things past which can't be changed or corrected: 30 per cent
Needless stress about our health: 12 per cent
Petty, miscellaneous stress: 10 per cent
Real and legitimate stress: 8 per cent

In perspective, the vast majority of things we get stressed about are not worth getting stressed about! It is also vital that we have an eternal perspective on our situations:

I consider that our present sufferings are not worth comparing with the glory that will be revealed in us. (Romans 8:18)

When I have a tough time and get stressed I try to reason with myself. I mentally jump out of the situation and look at it from the point of view of an onlooker – and it never looks as bad from that perspective. No matter how stressful I feel a situation is, time tells me that it was never as bad as I thought! If we jump to the heavenly perspective that God has and look through his eyes, our stress is really not that bad at all.

The promise of God in stressful times

> Blessed is the man who perseveres under trial, because when he has stood the test, he will receive the crown of life that God has promised to those who love him. (James 1:12)

God offers a promise, an encouragement and a hope for us when we endure stressful times. If we can just manage to keep on going, we will receive a reward in heaven that will be better than playing on any games console, winning any football match, getting any qualification or job and, dare I say it, better than going out with the nicest girl. Bro, keep going!

Don't get me wrong. I know that stress is tough. I have been through some very stressful times in my life and there are instances that are not under our control, such as bullying, and for those who are abused the stress is understandably immense. But whatever the cause of your stress, I am confident that if you use the principles of purpose, prayer, perspective and promise then you will deal with stress in a way that will help you become more of a rad lad. Start to deal with stress in a godly way today.

Sort it out

- Make a list of things that really get you stressed. Now go to God and tell him – he wants to know what makes you feel this way.
- Think about your own actions that cause you stress. How

can you eliminate these?

- Think about the things you find stressful that you do not need to stress about at all. Put these things into perspective, spend time with God and see the situations through his eyes.
- Take a look at the apostle Paul in the book of Acts in the New Testament and spend some time looking at the stressful situations that he got into. How did he respond?

Big bruva

God promises to give a crown of life to those who persevere under trial. Chat to your big bruva, who will probably have more experience of dealing with stress. Ask him how he copes and how he gives over his stress to God. (That might challenge him, so be sensitive here!) Explain to your big bruva the stressful situations you are going through and ask him to pray through these things with you. Ask your big bruva how to cope with stress in a godly way as you encounter it. Discuss together the Bible's promise of a crown of life and get excited about it!

Christians shouldn't be stressed! Christians shouldn't be depressed! I spent so many years thinking this and looking down on Christians who were stressed or depressed, yet it is an illogical reasoning that takes us there.

When I left school I decided to dodge university and get a job instead. I chose to be a waiter in Manchester and quickly learnt how to make a fortune – I made a lot of money from tips! I always had cash in my pocket and thought I was rich, but I was soon living beyond my means and ended up in debt. I got married and thought I could handle it. My wife had just qualified as a solicitor and would be earning soon. We had our first child and then our second, and all the time the debts grew and grew and we paid more and more interest. It didn't take long before I got to hate the postman coming, or the phone ringing. I used to feel physically sick and have panic attacks. I now worked in retail and was climbing the ladder, trying to earn more money to pay off more debts, and then we had our third child. This tipped me over the edge. My wife had also been struggling quite a lot as she was trying to hold down a full-time job and look after two young children, and her salary went on childcare.

It was no surprise to the doctor that I was showing signs of stress. Anyone would! In this crazy world, the more time-saving gadgets and the faster computers we have, we actually end up having less time to relax. Stress isn't a failure; it's a result of the times we live in. My doctor told me something had to give. I couldn't give up on my wife, my children needed looking after, we needed to move house as we had outgrown it, and we did need a new car. The only thing that could give was work, and so I was off work again. This was the exact answer, because my life at that moment came down to priorities, and work lost. We turned to God and dealt with the problem head on, and the stress went away. It might sound simplistic, but then it is. I think the question comes down to this: do we have the same priorities as the rest of the world, or do we put God first in everything? There will always be times of stress, that's the world we live in, but it is how we deal with it that sets us apart. Do we run away, or do we hand it to God and face it head on?

Adam Dyer, Youth Director YCC
www.urbanwarriors.org.uk

a final word . . .

The boys are on stage. The set-up is gritty, raw, real and edgy with drums, guitar and bass. The lights are shining on the lads, they are looking stunning and the crowd is waiting with bated breath. Soulcry are on stage ready, waiting, willing and wanting to do their thing. The boys launch into one of my favourite songs, 6/8 tune, T.J.'s lyrics echo throughout the venue as the crowd go wild, and the words challenge those who hear to commit themselves to a deeper level in their lifestyle: 'But I've got something, something inside, something I know that could save your life.' A great set is played and all have had a good night. The crowd leaves the venue buzzing and as I walk off there is only one line that is resounding in my head and lingering in the air.

'But I've got something, something inside . . .' T.J.'s lyrics state it loud and clear. Jesus Christ lives inside us and, if we allow him to, he can change our lives. The effect of a changed life is that every person you encounter – friend, girlfriend, parent, lecturer, homeless guy on the street, and everyone else in between – is touched by something dramatic and powerful. They meet with the powerful presence of

God. God can only impact the people you meet if you allow him to. You need to sacrifice your life and change it. Becoming a rad lad in your Christian walk is both scary and exciting stuff. However, you will walk away from this book and one of two things will take place. You will be challenged. Your desire will be to become a rad lad in all areas of your life. This challenge could last a few days, a week or a month at most – then you will be back to your usual self. Or you will be challenged, you will realise that it will be hard work, but you will go for it with everything you have and all that you are. By doing that you will make lasting and significant changes in your life that will truly impact the lives of those around you. Bro, let God change you.

Never regret it

John and I were good mates. We were e-mailing each other daily, getting to know what was going on in each other's lives, our likes, our dislikes, our aims and our desires. John was terminally ill with cancer and things went from bad to worse. We continued e-mailing each other in between his trips to the hospital, endless sessions of being pumped with drugs to ease the pain, and a lot of sleep. John knew that his life was slowly fading and wanted to die in the comfort of his own home. John amazed me: he was 18, and while I was blatantly gutted that he was dying, this rad lad had time to reflect on his life so far and whether he had lived it to the full. The last e-mail I got from him brought me to tears: 'I have lived for 18 years and as I look back I regret not living a lifestyle that was all out for God. I have messed up and I have got things wrong. There were things I did that didn't honour God but I chose to continue doing them. I wish I hadn't. If I regret many things at the age of 18 I don't want you to look back when you are 60 and recount a lifetime of regret. If something needs changing, change it. If you have dreams for God, chase them. It is in our changing and in our dreaming that God can change the world.' John died a few days later. Bro, if you have dreams for God, don't regret what you could have done. Change your life, pursue him and see lives around you touched and changed.

Eternity

Have you seen *Gladiator*? Maximus is stirring an army for battle and at the height of his speech he proclaims, 'Brothers, whatever you do in life echoes in eternity.' How true those words are. Dude, what are you reaping? You will have been engaged in sin – you may be sleeping around, lying, drinking too much or getting involved in anything else that doesn't please God, and it may seem that things are going from bad to worse. What you do in life echoes in eternity as well as now and in the future on this planet. You can have an impact at three levels, for good or for bad.

Level 1 – This life. Jesus died so that we could have life in abundance (John 10:10). By continuing in your sin you are not entering the fullness of life that Jesus died for you to have. Sinfulness is holding you back, and you can either seek to change and live your life out to the full, or you can remain where you are!

Level 2 – Future generations. The sin that you are entangled in affects those around you, for the worse. What about how your sin will affect your wife, your children, your grandchildren? How will your sin affect your descendants after you are long gone?

Level 3 – Eternal life. What the unsaved see! If Christians profess a lifestyle and don't live it, this hypocrisy pushes a dying world further away from the only person that can bring their life real meaning – Jesus. If our lifestyles mean that people enter eternity without knowing God then we will have to answer for it.

I want what you do in life to have a positive echo in eternity. I want to stir an army of rad lads who will not put this book down and forget it but who will accept the challenge that God has for their lives to become more like Jesus in love and grace with the help of the Holy Spirit, fulfilling everything that God has planned for them. If we accept this challenge then we, together, have a dramatic and far-reaching positive effect. Our lives will have an echo throughout eternity, and on this earth long after we are gone. Dude, it is now down to you.

Respect to rad lad

To be honest I am just a kid, 18 years of age, but I have a dream. My dream is to be used by God in order to see his kingdom come, right across the UK. I find things tough: I lust after girls, I am rude to my parents, I don't honour God in my homework and I could do with some advice on how to deal with my anger. I am a bit of a rough kid on a council estate in London, stuck in some bad ways. But I am a Christian and God has called me to change this council estate, to change the UK and to change the world – for him. I was involved in gangs – I stopped. I used to carry a gun around – I stopped. I used to swear – I stopped. And who is noticing the difference? My mates! When they ask why, I tell them. I am still trying to change and become better, but if my mates need help or advice, they come to me. Many have asked me to pray for them too. I have met with Jesus and what I have in him is greater than the swearing, lying, stealing, the guns or the sex. I have a relationship with an awesome God. If you are reading this thinking 'whatever', let me ask you: do you have a relationship with Jesus?

I figure that us lads could be used by God to change the world. If I work towards my character being more like the character of Jesus and impact my community, and you do the same with yours, we will change the world in a dramatic way. You are the one who has to want it, though, and it will only work if you are engaging with God. Now get before God and get on with it!

Steven Murphy, London

walk like Jesus walked

Mark Bowness is the founding facilitator of *walk like Jesus walked* (in association with Yeovil Community Church). WLJW facilitators speak at churches, youth events, festivals and conferences in order to mobilise an army to walk like Jesus walked.

walk like Jesus walked also produce a radical lifestyle/discipleship magazine for the youth of the UK. *thewalk* received pre-orders of 40,000 copies and goes out to events, youth groups and festivals across the UK. WLJW have also launched *Benchmark*, in order to meet the demands for a similar magazine aimed at the over thirties.

Mark and his wife Vikki are exploring relational church and are seeking to develop models of the church communities found in Acts, a church that went into 'all the world'.

For further information on the work of *walk like Jesus walked* please check out www.wljw.org or e-mail mark@wljw.org

walk like Jesus walked
The GateWay
Addlewell Lane
Yeovil
Somerset
BA20 1QN
www.wljw.org
admin@wljw.org

Other Survivor books include . . .

Red Moon Rising by **Pete Greig** – 24-7 is at the centre of a prayer revival across the globe and this book gives a fantastic insight into what God is doing with ordinary prayer warriors.

Passion for Your Name by **Tim Hughes** – To read this book is to share in a journey of discovery, of truths encountered, principles gleaned, mistakes made and lessons learned. A valuable companion for all worshippers!

The Unquenchable Worshipper by **Matt Redman** – This book is about a kind of worshipper. Unquenchable. Undivided. Unpredictable. On a quest to bring glory and pleasure to God, these worshippers will not allow themselves to be distracted or defeated. They long for their hearts, lives and songs to be the kind of offerings God is looking for.

Diary of a Dangerous Vision by **Andy Hawthorne** – The exciting story of the Message combined with crucial reflections and biblical teaching to equip you to run the race.

The Heart of Worship Files by **Matt Redman** – This book features highlights from the very popular website, heartofworship.com. Compiled by Matt Redman, it will encourage and inspire you to help others reach new depths of worship.

survivor

Facedown
by Matt Redman

"When we face up to the glory of God, we find ourselves facedown in worship."

FACEDOWN worship always begins as a posture of the heart. It's a person so desperate for the increase of Christ that they find themselves decreasing to the ground in acts of reverent submission. A soul so captivated by the Almighty that to bend low in true and total surrender seems the only appropriate response.

Bestselling author of *The Unquenchable Worshipper*, Matt Redman takes us on a journey into wonder, reverence and mystery.

FACEDOWN the album is now available on CD and DVD.

Wasteland?
by Mike Pilavachi

Are you looking for greater depth in your Christian life? Tired of the consumer model of spirituality? Are you ready to do the *right* things, even when things are going *wrong*? Feel like investing in obscurity . . . ? Mountain tops can be invigorating, but there's growth in the valleys. God says, 'Meet me in the desert.'

'Mike Pilavachi draws on his own experience and the Bible to infuse faith, hope and love in us, and to inspire us on our journey.' (J. John, Philo Trust)

survivor